BEFORE I KNEW

A Village Boyhood on Vancouver Island

Scott Brian Montgomery

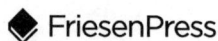

◆ FriesenPress

Suite 300 - 990 Fort St
Victoria, BC, V8V 3K2
Canada

www.friesenpress.com

ISBN
978-1-03-910874-5 (Hardcover)
978-1-03-910873-8 (Paperback)
978-1-03-910875-2 (eBook)

1. BIOGRAPHY & AUTOBIOGRAPHY, PERSONAL MEMOIRS

Distributed to the trade by The Ingram Book Company

"A boy's story is the best that is ever told."

—*Charles Dickens*

I dedicate this novel to my wonderful wife, Nooshin, who responded to my declaration that I was "going downstairs to my office to write my first book," with a paroxysm of laughter.

"We all live in a little village."

—*Patrick McGoohan*

I

We had voluminous snowfalls in winter during the 1960s. It was as if the Vancouver Island village of Sunderland, located uphill about seven kilometres from the ocean shore hamlet of Alston, was hit with a form of hurricane that dumped energy straight downward as heavy, heavy snow. Fifty to sixty centimetres overnight was not unusual. And, of course, just about everything could be shut down for several days until the winter rain washed the snow away. But during those days of snow . . . we frolicked.

I can remember Mother phoning the village office, reporting how many cars she had seen attempting the hill in front of our house, failing of course, and slipping backward down the hill. Many times her calls did the trick. A backhoe equipped with huge chains on its rear tires would soon appear and create a metre-high wall of snow at the foot of the hill, closing it off to vehicles. The children of Sunderland had their hill then, and those were the best of days during winter.

From morning until dark, we tobogganed and sledded to our hearts' content. At least I felt that way until my home-knit wool mittens, caked with frozen snow and ice, were no longer able to keep my hands warm. But I lived only a few short steps from halfway up the hill. I would scamper up the icy steps leading to our veranda and enter the house through the kitchen door. Onto the heating register the frozen mittens would go and I would replace them with a dry pair. I may have missed a few runs down the hill, or perhaps a spectacular toboggan wipeout, or someone slipping and banging his head on the frozen road, but that was all right. There would be more to come.

Playtime for my year older brother Calvin and I would be interrupted for lunch. Mother always made the same call: "STUEY . . . CALVIN . . . lunch is ready." Followed moments later by, "STUART AND CALVIN MOORE, COME INSIDE NOW. IT'S LUNCHTIME!" We knew then it was time to make tracks for home.

I don't know the exact conditions conducive to the production of icicles. I suppose it involves freezing and melting, repeated over and over again to produce the big ones. One appeared over time from the eavestrough above the outside cement steps leading to our basement door. We watched it grow every day. For safety's sake, my father wanted to knock it down, but my brother and I pleaded with him to let it grow. Eventually, it must have been almost two metres long with a diameter much larger than my waist at the time—even larger than my father's. Finally, I suppose my father's prayers were answered, because one evening as we sat around the kitchen table for our dinner, the icicle came down with a loud crash onto the cement steps, shattering, without any life lost.

Those were such great days. The freshness of the snow, the brightness of clear winter days; it made me feel alive. Mother Nature bestowed her gifts over and over.

· · ·

When not sledding, we attempted ice skating down at Sabatini's pond, which was just off the old railway grade on the way to the lake. It was a long walk over the grade—very tiring if there happened to be a lot of snow and it was necessary to break trail. The long shoestrings on our skates were ideal to suspend the skates from around our necks, but eventually they'd dig into our necks and shoulders. Often we were frozen by the time we finally sat down to put on our skates.

The ice on the pond was rough. Nearer the pond's edge we had to watch for bullrush leaves that broke the surface of the ice. If a skater hit one of those at top speed, he could have a serious wipeout. I can't recall spending too much time at the pond . . . ever. We usually got too cold; hot chocolate at home seemed a better option.

Wherever we went on wintry days, our village rewarded with beautiful views. The village itself was surrounded by round, snow-capped mountains, which to the east became a band of sharper mountains that formed a spine down the centre of Vancouver Island. Douglas fir trees dominated the vegetation. Indeed, they grew like weeds in the moist climate. I laughed out loud when I first heard our locale called a rain forest. But later I discovered in a geography book that it was, indeed, a rain forest.

Those fir trees produced an indelible mark in my mind. Once on a trip to sunny San Diego for a winter's getaway, I just felt something was missing as I drove my rental car past Christmas lights strung up on buildings and palm trees. It was the silhouette of the fir tree. Without them, Christmas seemed out of place.

• • •

In the winter months, Mum and Dad journeyed down from our mountain village to the nearby city of Clifton to curl. Calvin and I had no real understanding of exactly what curling was, and I'm quite sure that our sister Lena, who was five years younger than me, had even less knowledge. We knew that one evening a week,

Dad would put on his team's patterned Indian sweater, Mum would don her warm red jacket, and they would both procure their special brooms and special black knit gloves. I still have photos of my mother with her three teammates and my father with his. They are standing, leaning on their brooms for some reason. I could never determine what the game involved from the photos.

I was confused. Dad said that curling was a sport. For the life of me, I couldn't figger out how a sport could be played wearing that wool Indian sweater of his. It was so heavy. The one time I pulled it off its bent hanger and tried it on, I was itchy and hot within minutes. There was no way I could ever play baseball or soccer wearing an Indian sweater. I hoped no coach would ever select it as a uniform for kids.

Dad later explained that since curling was played on ice, he loved his sweater because it kept him nice and warm. He said he bet I didn't know that Indian sweaters were very famous and their heavy knit design was actually developed on Vancouver Island by the Cowichan indigenous people.

I emphasize that my parent's curling gloves were special because we were never allowed to use them. My father's would have been of little use anyway. They were much too big. He'd grown up on a farm. He explained that the work on a farm gives a person big hands. I have a smaller version of his hands, complete with abundance of hair.

Years later, when travelling on a school bus carrying my Grade 5 students and a class of kindergarten children, I was sitting next to a five-year-old boy. He kept looking at my hands. Finally, he piped up, "Mr. Moore, are you trying to grow a beard on your hands?"

My mother's gloves fit me reasonably well the one time I snuck a try-on. Most of the time, the curling gloves were kept rolled in a ball with their mate on the top of the fridge. It seemed a safe place since we kids couldn't see what was on that lofty spot. The top of the fridge was our Mount Olympus. We knew that special things inhabited the place, but we had little knowledge of them.

As pre-teenagers my friends and I took to, "hitching," when the roads were covered with compressed icy snow, making them as slippery as a skating rink. We would hide out near a stop sign, ideally behind a parked vehicle. When a car stopped, we would scurry out, keeping as low as possible, and grab on to the car's bumper. Sometimes the driver of the car knew that we were there, but he'd give us a ride anyway. We would get a tow for as far as the car would go within the village. What a time! Legend has it that I, Stuey Moore, once hitched a school bus all the way to Clifton.

I don't think I would ever have been described as an inherently bad child; I prefer mischievous. I will leave you to your opinion.

One time, I was in a hurry to join my friends and couldn't find my gloves. It was almost impossible to hitch without gloves, since in those days bumpers were made out of metal and very, very cold in freezing temperatures. My friends were on the veranda of my house, pleading with me to hurry up. I confess what I did. Pulling a kitchen chair over to the fridge, I stepped up and took my mother's curling gloves. But I knew I would return them soon.

The first few hitches went well. We were having so much fun. Well into a hitch, one by one my friends lost their balance and let go. Left alone on the ride, I soon hit a piece of ice with one of my boots. My feet went out from underneath me and I became out-stretched, still holding onto the bumper but being dragged along. I tried hard to get back up into hunched position. I soon realized that I couldn't. I vividly remember letting go, feeling my body slow down as I watched one of my mother's special black curling gloves retain its grip on the car's bumper and eventually disappear down the road.

Upon returning home, I made the biggest ball I could out of my mother's one remaining glove and placed it on top of the fridge. I never did hear anything about a missing curling glove.

I do know that in the years to follow there were a few other times when items went missing from the top of the fridge. Again, I confess. I have direct knowledge of a rather large, horrible-tasting cigar that was given to my father upon the birth of a friend's baby, having somehow mysteriously gone missing from Mount Olympus.

II

I imagine my parents were first interested in our family home because of its location halfway up the hill (we called it Hospital Hill) on First Street, at the top of which, if one went right for half a block, sat the hospital. You see, my father was a doctor, and he wanted to be close to the hospital. The senior doctor in the village, Dr. Ricks, actually lived right across the street from it.

Many a time when I was very young, my mum would send me to the hospital to retrieve my father for supper. Mrs. Coverdale, head nurse, she of soft Irish accent, would query whether I was there to see the newborn babe. My father would take me to the nursery and lift me up to peer through the window at the newly born child. In retrospect, I suppose he was trying to teach me about the wonder of life and, in his own way, encourage me to follow in his footsteps and become a physician.

The fact was, I couldn't really consider the profession. If I only had a dollar for every time in my childhood I was asked, "Are you going to be a doctor like your dad?" . . . It was a bit of a shame, I suppose, because I did seem to have an aptitude for science. I recall shocking Jack Walston in junior-high science class. We were to get our things ready for a chemistry test.

Jack called to me, "Moore, you idiot. Get your periodic table out. You need it for the test." I hadn't realized at the time that I had memorized the valences of all the elements and I assumed everybody else had as well.

I went on to win the science award in Grade 10. I still have it on a bookshelf. It's the Life book, *The Physician.*

. . .

Dad's chosen transport was a red 1964 Volkswagen Beetle ("The People's Car"). I think he loved the practicality of it and, of course, the modesty that it projected, since he was a modest man.

The Beetle was reliable and at times a real advantage for getting around snowy roads. Prior to the commonality of four-wheel drive vehicles, its rear-motor-over-the-drive-wheels produced good traction on slippery roads. I recall my Saturday-morning job delivering groceries for Maffetti's Grocery when I was 16. While I drove their Volkswagen van, similarly equipped with rear motor over the drive wheels, Cal was delivering for Cheung's Grocery, in their not-motor-over-the-drive-wheels Ford van. On a snowy wintery day, I'd be out delivering and see my brother stuck in the snow, cursing as I'd drive by with all the traction in the world, or at least all the traction that was necessary to avoid getting stuck on the streets of Sunderland. I'd slow down, honk my horn, and wave, with the kind of smile on my face that a brother knows means, "I win!"

Cal and I hadn't always been so competitive. Mum said we were inseparable when we were toddlers. And we had our own language before we knew English. Mum loved to tell the story about when Cal was in the raspberry patch. She told me to call my brother. I crawled across the kitchen floor to the open doorway and called out, "Arrraggooohool." In short order, Calvin's head became visible between the raspberry plants.

"Arraggooohool," he answered and then strode towards the house.

Dad stayed a loyal Volkswagen customer for years. After the red Beetle came a white one, and then a fastback and, finally, a Dasher when Dad was close to retirement and he and Mum lived south of Alston.

The Dasher was a precursor to the Rabbit and was a front-wheel-drive sedan. It was quite good in the snow, but when a new snowfall had occurred it was no match for the short, steep hill that started the drive up from the Island Highway in Alston to Sunderland. On one particular morning, Dad had to get to the medical clinic in Sunderland to see patients. He'd made two tries at the hill before returning home to retrieve me (I think I was home for the holidays from university).

"I need more weight over the wheels," he said. Apparently, I was going to be that weight.

Sure enough, when we got close to the bottom of the hill, he pulled over. I was instructed to lie on the hood and hold on tightly just below the windshield wipers. Dad took a good run at the hill. I could hear the front wheels spinning as he turned on to the hill, and I could see the determination on his face since my face wasn't far from his, just on the other side of the windshield. We made it! I thought the whole experience was fun, but Mum wasn't too pleased with Dad when I recounted the story.

I digress. That particular red Volkswagen Beetle seems central now to a number of stories.

I remember being asked by my father to accompany him on a house call (back in the day, doctors actually did house calls) when I was perhaps eight years old. Let me rephrase that. My mother *insisted* that my father take me with him, since that afternoon I'd caused commotion in the house, having fought with Lena once, and twice with Calvin. Mum had things to do other than referee.

Dad asked me to fetch his black medical bag from the hallway. I knew the spot. It was always there whenever Dad was home, although you couldn't see it, because it would be placed strategically behind his long overcoat, which hung to the ground, obscuring the bag from his children. It was a heavy leather bag, and it wielded a power over me. I felt anxious when the thought of sneaking a play with the bag came to me. I understood that it was one thing I had better not mess with—at all. Dad had reinforced that notion each time he'd given in to one of his children's pleadings and ceremoniously opened the bag to remove the necessary instrument to measure a skinny kid's blood pressure, or listen to a heart, or examine the inside of an ear. Inevitably, someone would be told there were potatoes growing in their ear canal.

I knew the doctor's bag had importance. Thor had his hammer. Dad had his doctor's bag. I'd seen in the comics how upset Thor would get if someone tried to mess with his hammer. It was the same thing with Dad and his bag.

I had to use two hands to carry the bag to the Beetle.

At the time, I felt special. Not only was I with my dad, who often worked long hours and was therefore absent from the family home a lot, but I was led to believe that I could be of help to him. And so you can appreciate my disappointment when I was told to wait in the Beetle and not go into the patient's home to assist my father in some form of doctoring.

There are only so many times an attentionally-challenged youngster can twist a car's steering wheel back and forth before becoming bored. And while I expected to be happy forever once I crawled over into the driver's seat, alas I was not. I distinctly remember the pleasure from pushing on the large round horn in the middle of the steering wheel. It wasn't a loud horn like the one in Mr. Renzo's big Ford Galaxy, but it sufficed, and I soon got into what I felt was a pleasant rhythm. My enjoyment was interrupted when my father hurriedly exited the patient's home and jogged to the car. It wasn't the first time—and you know what follows— that I was given a harsh speaking to. My score in the "Positive

Interactions with Family Members," column was less than satisfactory that day.

. . .

I must have been a little too immersed in the fantasy world of Bond, James Bond, because one night I hatched a scheme to take the Beetle for a midnight drive as some sort of special mission. I was about twelve years old. I'd driven before. Well, at least Dad had let me steer the Beetle once we got out of the village proper, while on our way to feed the horses in the morning. Our barn was located not quite two kilometres out of town on the Alston Road. And, I'd actually driven the Beetle around the barnyard by myself a few times, after Dad had patiently taught me how to coordinate pushing the gas pedal while releasing the clutch.

My parents were away somewhere, and someone (a woman) was staying at our house to care for us children. I was so excited and credited myself for my secret agent planning abilities. I'd wait until everyone was asleep, especially that someone (woman), then sneak out of the house, open the garage door, and drive the Beetle all the way out to Sunderland Lake. Actually, it seemed at the time there was much more to the operation than that. Inevitably, each of those nights while my parents were away, I'd lie in bed, rehearsing over and over in my mind the steps of my plan, until I could no longer stay awake.

. . .

Shortly after getting his driver's license at age 16, Calvin inherited the Beetle. He would bomb around town following his friend Maxie Dougwell, who would lead in his blue Beetle, with occasional stops at the Home Store near Maxie's house to indulge in a fudgsicle or two. I believe Maxie set the record at five.

When Maxie souped up his Beetle by having the rear fender's flared (I don't know what the inspiration was), Calvin soon followed suit. Cal's were kinda neat, though, because they were left primer black. They really stood out on a red car. I'm sure he felt even more proud following Maxie around the village.

Once Cal and I were at Herb's Drive-In Burger Bar in Clifton, having an order of fries during our lunch break from high school. We were past taking the school bus from Sunderland downhill to Clifton for high school (grades 11 and 12) since Cal had a car. Anyway, I must have had my driver's licence by then because Cal let me swap seats with him. I guess he gave me permission to drive us the three kilometres down the road back to school after our lunch. It didn't happen, however.

Shortly after having his Beetle's fenders flared, Cal installed a little chrome steering wheel in her. It was cool. The chrome spokes leading out from the horn had a series of different-sized holes. Definitely an upgrade over the stock Beetle's lacklustre job. I had been absentmindedly sticking my fingers into the holes in the steering wheel while admiring my reflection in the chrome, when one of my fingers got stuck. I mean really stuck. Despite several attempts, I just couldn't get it out. I think Cal saw the opportunity to skip the afternoon of school before I did. We set off for home, with me twisting my arms around the steering wheel whenever we came to any significant turn. Somehow we made the ten-kilometre drive. I think we were in our driveway for about three seconds when Mum appeared on the veranda. Calvin explained the problem. Mum disappeared back into the house and returned with a glass containing some cooking oil, which she slathered on to my stuck finger.

"Try it now," she said.

I tried.

"Try it again," she said.

I tried again. No luck.

Finally she reached into the car, grabbed my hand with both of her hands, and yanked . . . HARD! My finger came free, still attached to my hand, accompanied by my screech. I noticed a little less skin on my finger in a couple of places.

"Back to school," she said, before I'd even finished hyperventilating.

"Get outta there," said Calvin. "I'm driving."

. . .

I'd heard a hilarious story one day at high school. I couldn't wait to get home to tell Mum, inserting myself as the main character.

"Mum, you're not going to believe what happened to me today. I went to Herb's for lunch. When the carhop brought me my burger, I could see a hair sticking out of the meat patty. I complained. The carhop told me not to complain to her because she didn't make the burgers. She suggested I could go talk to someone inside . . . so I did. When I complained to the person behind the counter, she also said I couldn't complain to her because she didn't make the burgers. She directed me down a hallway to a small room. Upon entering, I saw a big, fat, hairy guy wearing an undershirt. He grabbed a bunch of ground beef from a bowl, moved it from hand to hand, and then put it into his armpit, squeezing his arm down to compact the ground beef into a patty."

Not two seconds elapsed before Mum said, "You think that's bad? I was there last week and I found a hair in my doughnut!"

. . .

III

Oh I am languorous this morning. Often of late, I have an ache in my lower back or in my hips. Gone are the days when I can attribute the pain to some form of hard work the previous day. During this past year, sometimes I had a sharp pain on the right side of my chest or in my right shoulder. The doctor hypothesizes that it's Tietze Syndrome, some kind of inflammation at the point where the ribs attach to the breastbone. What a strange thing it is. Doctors are unsure of its cause and less certain of its treatment. It may disappear suddenly, only to reappear months or years later. It is at bay at the moment and I am thankful, for its pain is sharp and severe.

Recently, I had a telephone appointment with my doctor. I prefixed the conversation by asking where I should begin. I had several health concerns on my list. The doctor was short with me and suggested I tell him my main concern. I had little satisfaction from the appointment. I think the good doctor is older than I am, perhaps prone to many of the ailments that plague me, minus the hypochondria, I suppose.

Once, years ago, after scraping a hand on the sidewalk after an everyday-type wipeout on my bicycle, I bypassed my mother, the regular medical professional on duty, for my father who was home that day. I wanted a more educated opinion. After a quick examination, he diagnosed the problem as a case of "Dirtification" and it was prescribed that I go outside and play.

. . .

Pain, as you know, is largely absent for most during one's younger years. Wasn't it wonderful to move one's body without having to think of the immediate or delayed consequences?

My first sensation of pain—although it wasn't severe pain, more an uncomfortableness—was in the womb. I know what you're thinking. Most think it is absurd that I can remember this. However, I steadfastly maintain that I can.

The memory is from my birth. You see, my mother had a 48-hour long labour with me. Once again, I know what you're thinking. Forty-eight hours . . . that's absurd. But I heard the story many times and I don't think that's the sort of story a mother would make up.

I distinctly remember a darkish place with walls of light that moved or appeared to move as I suppose I was squirming about. And there was a sensation of constriction, that this previously comfortable place was now uncomfortably tight as I twisted and turned. I can see it all very clearly in my mind's eye.

My mother used to love telling the story that after my birth my head was in rather tough shape, having suffered from the use of forceps. Apparently, when one of mother's friends came to visit, she initially showed a degree of shock upon seeing me, but she quickly saved the day by saying to my mother, "Don't worry, he'll soon look better."

. . .

My father and mother came to Sunderland in 1955 after my father's graduation from medical school in Winnipeg, Manitoba. They were excited at the prospect of escaping Manitoba's brutal winters, and I suppose romanticized the idea of living on an island. Dad's first employer was the mining company; he soon settled in as the village's new young doctor, there to help share the load of elderly Dr. Ricks.

Dr. Ricks reattached the tip of the little finger on my right hand when I was about three years old. I'd stuck my finger into the crack of a folded tabletop, which my brother closed quickly, thus slicing off a portion of my fingertip and introducing me to the world of stitches. By all accounts, the old doc was a good fella, although I didn't think much of him at the time. I recall seeing him once when several of his fingers were bandaged up. My dad said his fingers had been deteriorating due to exposure to X-ray chemicals. It didn't sound pleasant.

Soon after my parents arrived, the coal-mining industry that had built the village was over. During my early childhood, the village suffered hard times, especially when the mines closed for good. Many of my friend's fathers turned to logging at camps up-island during the week, returning on weekends. Those men made decent money, but there were dads who didn't leave the village and were either unemployed or working at relatively poor-paying jobs. And, of course, among the men there were a number left disabled from mine or logging injuries, some of which had taken to the bottle.

· · ·

SCOTT BRIAN MONTGOMERY

"Growing apart does not change the fact that for a long time we grew side by side; our roots will always be tangled. I am glad for that."

—Ally Condie

My first best friend in Sunderland was Cale Renzo, the son of an Italian-descended father and a Scottish-descended mother. They were good people. For a time during our elementary school years, Cale and I were inseparable.

We'd go to his house one school lunchtime and ask his mother if I could have lunch with them since my mother wasn't home . . . and then we'd repeat the same procedure at my house a few days later. We kept it going for a long time until one day the two mothers ran into one another at Clancy's Butcher Shop, the shop with the sawdust on the floor, where they simultaneously asked one another whether everything was okay! The jig was up.

Cale lived in an area of the village called "The New Houses." I think there were about 18 houses on two streets with an alley separating the homes. They were, of course, newer houses, but in retrospect I don't believe they were all that new, just newer than the late 1800s or early 1900s houses from the thriving days of the coal mines.

Many centurial homes still survive in Sunderland today. A few years back, I went to an estate sale at a typical old wood Sunderland home. Part of the sale was inside the home. I was shocked to see that the living room floor was actually dirt, with rugs thrown here and there. The foundations of these homes were built with wood, not cement. I suspect once water got under a house the wood floor would rot away relatively quickly.

Cale and I spent many afternoons riding our bikes back and forth between his place and mine. Those were the best times. At a certain time of the year we'd pull thorny green pods off a chestnut tree. If Cale had his pocket knife, he'd slice them open to get at the brown chestnuts. If not, we'd smash them down on the tarvy and tear them open with our hands. We'd attach two chestnuts together with a long string to make bolas. Then we'd swing them around and around trying to release them at just the right moment so they'd sail up into the air and wrap around the telephone wires that hung skyward along one side of every village street, suspended between sturdy telephone poles. Other times we'd construct bows and arrows out of young wild maple trees. That would take a long time. Often when it came time for the first test, the bow would snap. Ugh!

And, all the while, we'd keep an eye out for what the other kids in the neighbourhood were doing.

There were frequent games of "Guns." One of the older boys would divide us into two teams. Participants were required to have toy six shooters, tommy guns, or some other imitation of a deadly weapon that we regularly saw put to good use in television programs like *Combat*. We didn't have to go far to be in the forest. It was a perfect place to hone one's combat skills.

One day, Cale and I decided we were going to take up smoking. And while he was okay with scoffing one of his father's rolling papers, he greatly opposed the idea of dipping into the can of Player's Navy Cut cigarette tobacco, featuring the picture of a sailor's head. What were we to do? It came to Cale that in his father's tiny, detached workshop/shed there was a pencil sharpener that contained "tons of stuff that looks just like tobacco and must be pretty much the same thing." I don't know what credit I can give to never showing much interest in smoking after that experience, but I suspect some is due.

. . .

A few years later, I recall getting a shout from Cale that something was up. I ran over to meet him in the large, forested area between our house and the New Houses. The New House kids called it Moore's Forest. A rumour existed that my father, Dr. Moore, owned the forest.

There was Cale, along with Johnny Lafleur. About two years older than Cale and me, and approximately fifteen centimetres shorter, Johnny had a wry little smile on his face, which I later realized was a permanent feature. The look suggested he knew much about much, however it didn't take long to figger out that this cigarette-loving, alleged mini-Plato . . . didn't.

Johnny lived south of town, about halfway to Alston, in a no-man's land known as Skunk Hollow. There wasn't much there. A scattering here and there of houses. Monkey Deluca lived just down the road from Johnny. You didn't need to be Sherlock Holmes to figger out what he was known for; same for Horsehead Robinson, who lived a tad farther than Monkey.

Johnny Lafleur's house, it seemed to me, was a tiny white house on the edge of a large lot, where logging trucks were stored and repaired. He had several brothers and sisters. Dare I say there were a whole bunch of Les Fleurs?

There was a rather widespread tale that I'd heard prior to my introduction to Johnny . . . that he had driven one of the huge logging trucks up and down the logging road behind his house— when he was four years old! If you knew Johnny, you wouldn't doubt it. Although it must have been a physical miracle, since Johnny was the runt of his family. And that was saying something.

My mum recounted the story of meeting one of Johnny's little brothers.

She had driven down to Smiley Valley, which wasn't far out of town, to drop off hay and a salt block for some horses we had pastured there. I guess she was unloading the back of the truck when this little squirt rode up on his bike and asked what she was doing. My mom explained, all the while wondering what this kid, who looked to be about six years old, was doing riding around unsupervised.

He explained that he was looking for "something to do," and soon volunteered to help. He walked up to the salt block that my mum had just moved from the truck to the ground.

With an "I'll get this for ya," he placed his hands on the block and proceeded to lift.

Next came, "JESUS CHRIST . . . SON 'O BITCH IS HEAVY!"

Anyway, back to Moore's Forest. Johnny had had the genius to swipe his dad's cigarette-rolling machine and some strong Export A tobacco. I figgered I knew the plan: sit in the bush, make smokes, and smoke'um.

But Johnny had to add another level. And so we abandoned the camouflage protection of the forest and crossed the street into the school yard, where Johnny announced we should climb up on the Industrial Education Building to enjoy the "Catch of the Day."

Cale and I made short work of the climbing challenge. Johnny made it too, without the ladder I imagined he'd need.

And so we sat on the roof, Johnny assembling cigarettes like an old pro, in full view of anyone passing along First Street.

Ahhh, good times. I didn't much partake in the smoking. The tobacco was too strong. I think Cale had one cigarette. Johnny had two or three. Eventually, Cale and I just sat, taking in the wonderment of the miniature smoking legend.

Soon after, a passerby on the street shouted that he was going to report us. We fired a few choice curse words at him and then slunk back to the other side of the roof and descended.

IV

The King Charles Hotel was one of three reasonably rundown pubs within the two primary business-occupied blocks of Main Street. In later years when I went off to university (yes, I was known as one of the local boys who had, "gotten out"), a government liquor store was added. Ample libations were available for those of drinking age and so inclined of the 1,500 or so populace. Once when I dared to bring a university girlfriend home to show her my roots, on the drive through town she commented, "What do they do for excitement around here . . . rob the liquor store?" When we returned to Sunderland later that evening after a night out at the movies in Clifton, there were indeed two police cars with flashing lights parked in front of the liquor store!

Outside the King Charles and across the street was a great ambush location to work from on snowy winter nights. My friends and I would hide behind a two-metre high snow pile and go to work in the early evening preparing snowballs. It was such a lovely, wintry, peaceful scene prior to our offensive. The temperature had dropped. It was too cold to snow. No people walked the icy sidewalks. Just a rare car would pass down the street. It was, in general, so quiet that you could hear the snow crunch under your feet or under your legs if you chose to lie against the snowbank while preparing your ammunition. Under these calm conditions, one could be startled, and most definitely grossed out, should a comrade shoot a stream of snot out of their nose.

We waited as hunters do. Most often it would not be long before some poor sap would exit the Charles hurriedly to get home to "the wife." Big mistake! Three or four steps out of the door and he would be bombarded by a flurry of snowballs. Confused, he would scan the landscape across the street while covering his head with one arm. There would be little fight in him after a day's work and a belly full of Lucky Lager (none of those fancy-dancy craft beers in those days)! What energy was left, I'm sure, was saved to argue with his better half about why he'd stayed at the Charles for another round. Truly, it was a battle like the German's panzers rolling into largely unprotected Warsaw.

Sometimes a "You son of a bitches," would be thrown back at us, meant to wound. But it would not deter us from restocking our ammunition and implementing our next invasion. As victors, we reaped the spoils.

. . .

One empty lot up from the King Charles was the town pharmacy, now long gone. It was owned and operated by Mr. Randle, a nice enough bloke, generally very serious whenever he stood behind the counter at the back of his shop. My father and Mr. Randle were charged with managing the collection baskets at our church, the white United Church just down the hill and up the dip from our house. Every Sunday at some juncture, I can't remember when it was in the service, my father and Mr. Randle, dressed in their suits, would walk to the front of the congregation, retrieve a basket each, walk to the first row on their respective side of the centre aisle, pause, and then hand the basket to be passed from person to person down the bench seat. I saw coins and even dollar bills dropped into the baskets as they worked their way from hand to hand. My siblings and I would anxiously wait our turn until we would drop our parent-supplied nickel or dime into the basket. And so it went. My father and Mr. Randle would retrieve their baskets and then move on to the next row until all collections had been received. It seemed to me that my father was just as serious as Mr. Randle was throughout the whole process.

Dad always seemed to be serious when we were in church. For a time, Calvin and I attended an after-church boys' club: Sigma Cs. It was announced we would be having a special guest the following week—Dr. Moore, who would be speaking to us about growing up to be men. Part of me was proud that my father was considered an esteemed guest speaker. Another part of me was unsure of how my father's "birds and the bees" talk would go over with my peers.

I mean, my friends and I knew the basics. We'd heard about it from older boys in the neighbourhood. I was first exposed to the facts about two years earlier when my dad had given me the little booklet, "A Doctor Talks to a Nine to Twelve Year Old." Honestly, I was nauseous when the booklet got down to "brass tacks."

I couldn't do that, I'd thought. But little did I know that it wouldn't be long before, "doing that," would be on my mind a lot.

Dad came in later in our meeting the following week. He was given a nice introduction. He looked serious. He started reading aloud from a textbook. I don't think he lifted his eyes during the course of his presentation.

I just remember him reading," The male organ is about the size of a finger." I immediately looked down at the fingers on both my hands. What?

• • •

Mr. Randle's shop was the only one in the village that had a reasonable assortment of magazines, most of which I had classified as "irrelevant," in my preteen mind. But on that wall display, just inside the door of the pharmacy, to the right, was my interest: comic books. There was everything a boy my age loved and more. Superman, Batman, Hawkman, Aquaman, Sgt. Rock, and Archie (too much implied romance for me to be comfortable with between Archie and Veronica). A kid could spend a lot of time flipping through the pages of his favourite comic and evidently many did, as often an even more serious Mr. Randle would suddenly appear with the reminder that the comics in the store were for buying, not for reading. I'm pretty sure it was the kids who had just had a greasy lunch up the street at the Alder Cafe who ruined it for the rest of us. Their dirty fingers likely messed up quite a few comics and therefore spawned Mr. Randle's diligence to protect his merchandise.

I rarely left the store without spending my weekly ten cents allowance on a comic—usually Superman.

It's interesting how a fascination with superheroes was implanted years ago and how it manifests even today with my interest in the latest superhero movie. How valid an archetype must the superhero be in order to have spoken to boys from years ago and continue to speak to the boys of today?

And, by the way, who came up with the idea of a Batman vs. Superman movie? Any informed mind knows that Batman wouldn't stand a chance.

. . .

Across the street from the pharmacy was Stan's Barbershop. Stan was my second barber. Before my brother and I were old enough to attend school, Mum used to um . . . cut our hair. I recall that Dad had gone to Vancouver one weekend to attend a medical course. Calvin and I needed haircuts. I was first up. Things were proceeding well until I suddenly squirmed to one side, which resulted in my mum cutting a swath right across my head. There wasn't any way to fix it so she proceeded to give me a complete baldie. Next, Calvin was up. She gave him a baldie as well so it would appear to my father that the haircuts were by design. Upon returning from the big city, Dad wasn't impressed. Mum's barbering career was over.

Stan's shop seemed nice enough. There were usually a couple of men slumped in chairs watching Stan or his sidekick Reuben give a haircut. The conversation was mature talk from deep adult voices. By the time I was called up by Stan, I was already squirming around. Stan would plunk an upholstered board across the arms of his barber chair and I'd get a hoist up from him. He was a master at giving a decent cut to a kid that couldn't sit still. Cal was known as the behaving one. He most often was.

. . .

There was a story my mum used to tell about another time my dad was away in Vancouver on a medical course. It must have been a longer training because my mother had decided she was going to take on the challenge of the journey with two very young boys.

At the time my parents had some heavy, 1950s sedan with a "three-in-the-tree shifter" and a weird clutch. My mom was terrified of how things might go when she had to disembark from the Black Ball Ferry, once docked in Vancouver. She had a plan, however. She'd brought a doll with her, that she'd kept tucked away in her purse.

Cal and I were bouncing around in the back seat of the car—no car seats or seat belts in those days. Just as cars were unloading, Mum started the car, pulled out the doll, and said, "Look boys, something for you to play with," gently lobbing it into the back seat.

Seconds later, before she even had to move the car, the doll's head came flying over the front seat, followed by the doll's legs, etc.

She noted her plan didn't turn out to be all that helpful in managing her anxiety about driving off the ferry.

. . .

Our village shoe store, Earles, was an important shop, but alas, it too is gone. While I was still in elementary school, the footwear of choice for a boy were PF Flyers running shoes. These canvas, three- quarters high, flat-soled runners came in two colours: white and black; an improvement on Henry Ford's old adage, "You can get your Model T in any colour, as long as it's black." I can remember Mum buying me a pair of the whites. Soon thereafter, we both realized that they didn't retain their bright whiteness for very long! Therefore, blacks it would be in the future. Cal returned from a trip to Earles on one occasion with a green pair. A GREEN PAIR! He was the envy of many kids on the playground for days after that before, inevitably, a bully put him down, basically for being different.

In Grade 4, I joined the latest fad with a pair of three-quarter high, three-lace holes, black leather, pointed-toe "snoot" boots. I'd been coached by friends that it was important to get "Blakies" put on the heels of the shoes—those little flat metal thingamajigs that were probably for tap dance shoes. You felt cool and tough, clicking your way on a cement sidewalk or on a classroom floor. Your arrival was definitely noticed.

. . .

The Alder Café was also known as Sammy's. Sammy, who owned the café, was of oriental extraction. He was short and always wore a forever stained white cook's tunic, well-earned in a busy kitchen. He had a funny little cook hat, never centred on his head. I don't recall ever seeing him without a cigarette hanging out of his mouth, and usually the length of the ash on the end of it defied gravity.

You could get a 25-cent hamburger ("You get what you pay for") and a 15-cent order of fries. Sammy's secret ingredient was . . . grease. A Coke in one of those tall glass bottles would cost you 10 cents. And of course that concoction in those days contained an effective dose of caffeine . . . great for my already hyperactive disposition. Lunch for well under a buck! Do I need to work harder to seduce you into the romance of those days?

Speaking of romance . . .

Even as a kid, I knew Sammy was a smart businessman. He knew that diversification was the key to any business' success, and he knew his competition. He determined that there was an item that he could keep behind the counter . . . an item that young men would find much easier to purchase from him than stern-faced Mr. Randle, standing behind his pharmacy counter just a few doors down the street. And so when love was in the air, propagated by laughter and a shared order of Sammy's fries between a young man and young woman, the young man would trot over to Sammy who stood knowingly behind his counter, and whisper, "Sammy, can you sell me a rubber?"

Sadly, Sammy passed away quite young. Mrs. Sammy and her children continued to operate the café, but for the young men it just wasn't the same. Asking for what they really, really needed from Mrs. Sammy was just . . . awkward. And so, by necessity, Mrs. Sammy's 12-year-old son, Jerry, took up the stock in trade, managing the prized item kept behind the counter. With far from his late father's stoicism, Jerry would ask any inquiring customer, "Do you want one with a hole in it? They're cheaper."

• • •

There had once been a telephone pole located right outside the entrance to Sammy's. I have confirmed it. A few weeks ago, my wife and I went for a drive through Sunderland but no such telephone pole was to be found. I actually went into the Sunderland Museum photo archives to look for evidence that there had been a pole there. There was!

It seemed there was always someone leaning up against the telephone pole, having a smoke. I suppose that particular telephone pole had the best vantage point for viewing the main, "comings and goings" in the village. One of the more frequent pole-leaners was Dwayne Kalankski, aka "Klank." Klank was tall, hook-nosed, and a little older than my friends and me. He was the type of fellow who wouldn't hesitate to share how things worked with younger, impressionable children.

One late afternoon, Klank introduced a friend and I to the wonderful pastime of the "gobbing" game. Basically, under Klank's close tutelage, my friend and I were arranged in such a manner as an old-time duel would be, except we would be placed much closer together since our weapons did not possess the same range as pistols. We would square ourselves from about three metres. One would go first, then the other. If neither of our spitting attempts found fair purchase on our opponent, we would each take a step closer to one another and repeat the procedure. On it went until, well, you know. Like in golf, if you had a long game, you had the advantage.

I think we were in the early stages of a competition one day, under the close observance of our teacher, Klank, when my father happened to be driving by in his red Volkswagen Beetle. What followed was a talking to, an elaboration at length of acceptable versus unacceptable young gentlemanly behaviour when positioned in a public place. So ended my internship into the competitive world of the gobbing game.

V

Village life offered so much . . . well, besides the gobbing game. As a boy, you had freedom, and while I didn't think about it at all during that time, there was safety to that time and place.

My mother would think nothing of sending my brother or me on errands around the village. With my single-speed CCM bike, I could do the rounds in no time, but one had to learn the skill of kicking a dog if one chased you with the intent to bite. There were lots of dogs wandering around in those days. Years later I wrote a short story called, *The Dogs Don't Bark Anymore*. It was my lament to the days when I "felt" what was happening on a street, through sight and sound, as opposed to driving quickly from A to B in the mostly sterile atmosphere of an automobile interior.

There were lots of dog fights. You'd hear a shout, "Dog fight!" It was like receiving a special invitation to what you expected would be a great show.

I recall being sent to bicycle down to Mr. Clancy's butcher shop to pick up some porkchops for dinner. I coasted down the hill from our place and peddled up the dip towards the church when I heard the call: "DOG FIGHT!"

Halfway down the block towards Maffetti's, Round One was underway. Two good-sized dogs were sizing one another up. By the time I pedalled downhill to the spot, which was pretty much smack dab in front of Arthur Thompson's grandmother's house, a small crowd had gathered and the action was picking up. It became fierce. The dog's growled and nipped at one another as they went round and round like they were caught in a mini tornado.

In short order, I could see adults opening their front doors to see what the racket was all about. These were two strong young dogs and the battle raged on. Suddenly, the door flew open to the Alger's house and Mr. Alger came charging out, crossing the road, running up to the dogs with the intent of stopping the fight before one or both were injured.

He shouted at the dogs to no avail. Then making the decision to do what he believed necessary to end things he started swinging his right leg, trying to kick one or both of the combatants. The dogs just jumped sideways and continued their scrap. Mr. Alger must have taken five or six good kicks but could only find air. The crowd roared with laughter. We had come expecting a drama, but it turned out to be the best comedy we had seen in a while.

After a few more minutes, the battle ceased. I don't think a victor had been decided nor were the dogs exhausted. It might have been the case that they felt sorry for Mr. Alger.

The crowd soon broke up after several members of the audience had completed their reviews of the fight and Mr. Alger's comedy routine. I continued on my bicycle to the end of the block, stopped as I should at the stop sign there (opposite Maffetti's Grocery), and continued on to the main street, from where I could see Mr. Clancy's shop.

It was a busy place. It must have been late afternoon. Many adults were entering the shop to get hamburger meat, steak, pork-chops, or sausages for their evening meal. As I entered, I could detect the familiar scent of the sawdust shavings that covered the entire wood floor. The line moved fast. Soon I was handed the usual brown-paper-wrapped soft package of porkchops, which had already been recorded on my mother's account.

Long after the butcher shop disappeared from Sunderland, I puzzled over the purpose of the sawdust on the floor. It was certainly annoying if you got it into your shoes or stuck in your socks. I later learned the sawdust was used to absorb grease, fat, and blood.

With the package of chops in one hand and my other hand choking on one handlebar grip, I set off. A half block or so up, I turned right just past Mr. Beck's candy store and started up First Street for home.

When I'd gone almost a block, I heard someone wailing. I continued on towards the sound. Right by the white church was Bobby Flynn. He was on top of someone, pushing his head into the sidewalk. I shouted at Bobby and he released his hold. Up jumped Jack Walston, with a huge goose egg on one side of his forehead. Bobby was obviously incensed. I don't know what had happened. Neither Bobby nor Jack were in the mood to chat. Like a couple of dogs that were done, they walked off in opposite directions. I coasted down the dip and made it almost halfway up Hospital Hill to my house with two or three pedal strokes.

. . .

It seemed to me that the village was rather uniformly composed of people with similar ethnic backgrounds and origins. Was that really the case? Or as a child, did I just not think about it? Maybe I thought we were all the same because we were all villagers of Sunderland. Yes, that's it. That's the way I looked at it back then.

I knew Mr. Beck was from Hungary, and good buddy Foo Cheung was of Chinese ancestry. Slush and his little brother Muzzy had a funny last name. Mr. Maffetti and his clan were Italian—there were a lot of Italians in Sunderland. Everyone knows that Italians breed like rabbits . . . (I'm just kidding, Mr. Francolini! No need to phone me)!

The rest of the population, by bulk, were of Anglo-Saxon stock.

If you rode your bicycle down past the old Sunderland Recreation Institute, and made a quick left before continuing straight on to the part of town known as Camp, you would reach the old railroad grade. Back in the day, steam locomotives pulled cars of coal, which had been extracted from nearby mines, down to Empire Bay for export all over the world. In my day, there was hardly any evidence that trains had travelled the path, just the odd rotten piece of wood sleeper that the steel rail had laid on, perhaps a railway spike. It was a good path to travel on, since it was generally level compared to a lot of streets about the village.

Past Camp were the remains of Chinatown. There wasn't much left of what had been rumoured to be, sometime prior to the Second World War, the second-largest Chinatown in North America, next to San Francisco's. With shovels in hand, my friends and I spent many a day digging for old Chinese pots and opium bottles, trading them in for a dollar or two from a man who I'm sure made a pretty penny out of the deal.

There were many out-of-towners who drove too quickly through Camp on their way to dig at Chinatown; lots of Americans. Tragically, a youngster was hit by a car in Camp and killed. Camp resident Marion Corbin, she of beauty and brains, joined several others to protest. The residents advocated hard for a solution to the dangerous volume of cars that were streaming through the narrow road of Camp. The village council responded. Not long after, a paved road around Camp was created, pretty much on top of the old railway grade. On the far end of Camp, a barrier was put in place, closing the road off to through traffic and likely preventing further tragedy.

Now if one continued along the old railway grade past Chinatown you'd come to towns with now-cringe-inducing names, Japtown and then Coontown. There certainly wasn't anything remaining in my day, except perhaps the odd crab apple tree, whose apples more than likely would give you a stomach ache and ruin at least part of your day if you happened to be riding onward to the lake for a day of swimming fun.

Most of the inhabitants of these "towns" had been largely employed in the coal mines back in the day or had laboured on the railroad's construction. Their contribution cannot be overestimated.

And so, evidently there was quite a mix of culture and race back in the early days of Sunderland. I didn't think about it back then. I don't think I ever knew a person of Japanese descent while growing up. And I certainly didn't see any black people. I do recall a story about a black person, however.

On the outskirts of Sunderland along the road to Clifton, there was a small gas station known as the Home Store. It had just two gas pumps, and there was a small store area that sold a few necessities. At the back of the store and up three steps was access to the home of the proprietor family, the Norgaards. Another funny last name to me, which my father attempted to explain by telling me they were Danes. It took me awhile to figger that one out, as the only Dane I had ever come across was the Great Dane that woofed and jumped on the tall fence at the back of Mr. McKellar's yard, whenever anyone walked down the alley behind his house. I guessed that the Norgaards were just regular Danes and not great ones.

Anyway, Will Norgaard (aka "Norgy"), a classmate of my brother's, had a large black dog named Blacky. Norgy would regularly forget to let Blacky back inside the house after he was outside doing his business. I mean Blacky did his business outside. As far as I know, Norgy used the facilities inside the house.

Mr. Norgaard (Norgy Senior) would get quite frustrated with Norgy because Blacky would knock over the garbage can in front of the entrance to the store or otherwise annoy customers while they were getting gasoline.

On one particular day, the stars must have been in alignment for a fluke event to unfold.

Just as Norgy Senior walked up the few steps at the back of the store to shout for Norgy to get Blacky back into the house, a black man pulled in to fuel his car.

Norgy went to the side door of the house and called out, "Blaaaaaacccccccckkkkkkkyyyyyyy." Which surely got a reaction from the customer simply hoping to fuel his car without incident.

Apparently Blacky didn't care to be interrupted in his outside exploration and so Norgy repeated his call: "Blaaccckkkyyy."

The customer grew more uncomfortable.

Blacky did not respond.

Finally, out of frustration and with a sense of urgency, Norgy let out a very staccato shout, "BLACKY! YOU GET YOUR BLACK ASS IN HERE!"

Legend has it that the customer paid in a hurry and left. I wonder if the man ever told anyone of his experience and, if so, how could it not be a mark against Sunderland. Perhaps the perception was passed on that Sunderland was a very racist place, however I do not recollect that it was, although I am speaking solely through my experience.

VI

*"Candy is childhood, the best and bright moments
you wish could have lasted forever."*

—Dylan Lauren

To me, and I'm sure to most kids at the time, the focal point of what I shall call "Upper Downtown," was Beck's candy store. Two-and-one-half blocks from our house, near the top of main street, was an old rundown shop that contained a plethora of CANDY. Above the entrance was an ancient sign that identified the establishment as once one "Golden Urn," but its days of golden were long gone. Upon entering, a large empty space took up most of the left half of the room. A length of tables end to end reached pretty much all the way down to a woodstove from bygone days. The tables on your left and the wall to the right effectively funnelled you into the far-right corner of the room. There would be no objection to this funnelling because as you approached the end of the room on the right were shelf upon shelf of large jars containing every kind of candy you could imagine.

Mr. Beck! Yes, Mr. Beck would appear from a back room wiping his hands on a towel, asking in his Hungarian accent, "Can I help you?"

You could do a lot of damage with 10 or 15 cents. Jars were labelled one cent each, two for one cent, even three for one cent. The man was a marketing genius! Yet the personal service was labour-intensive, involving the opening of jar after jar. You'd make your choices by tapping the jar, since in most cases you didn't know the names of the candies. After choices were made, Mr. Beck's big fingers would dig in to separate the candies, and then he'd expertly shake the jar to deposit the precise number of candies requested into his palm. Then he'd screw the lid back on. Mr. Beck was always cheerful and helpful. My favourites were the round red-hot candies. Yum.

My father told me that Mr. Beck had put his son through medical school by toiling for many years in that store. I admired Mr. Beck even more when I heard that. I'd heard what a financial struggle it had been for my father to go from the farm to completing his own medical education.

Years later, at age 15, I dropped into Mr. Beck's store to buy a pop. I told him that I was going to Germany as part of a Rotary exchange program. He offered to help me out since he had a working knowledge of the German language.

He continued with something like, "You may need this with a young lady. *"Haben zee goot guhrschlopen?"* Translation: "Did you sleep well?"

For the record, while I did memorize the phrase . . . just in case . . . I didn't have the opportunity to use it. The only time I was in the game and it looked like I might get to first base with a German girl, the mission was aborted because I made a fool out of myself on account of having chugged a couple of beers, purchased from a pop machine at a gas station. In retrospect, my question, "Do you know you can buy beer in pop machines in Germany?" should have been left out of my speech to the Rotary Club upon my return from the trip.

Across the street from Mr. Beck's was the once majestic Royal Theatre. For years it sat with the windows boarded up. Many will know that later it would become a long-operating auction house. I myself bought a beautiful antique oak bed at one Friday evening auction. Many containers of good solid wood antique furniture came there for auction from Wales and other parts of Britain.

Along with several friends, I remember breaking into the Royal during its boarded up years, under the tutorage of some older boy . . . can't recall who.

We walked through the main foyer and thumped around in the dark on the sloping floor where movie seats once afforded patrons a good view of the movie screen. There was no screen left, but there was a stage. Up on the stage to one side, Gumper (more about him later) found an old fire extinguisher and, in true vandal spirit, managed to activate the damn thing and soak most us.

Back up the sloping floor through the left entrance to the foyer, we climbed up some stairs. We were surprised upon reaching the little room at the top to discover that there was still a big, old movie projector all set up, though I'm sure it had been years upon years since it had last seen use. I wonder if there is anyone alive today who ever attended a movie at the elegant Royal Theatre. That would be a story!

An empty lot uphill from the Royal was the mysterious Masonic Hall. My father belonged to the Masons for years and yet we kids never knew what went on there. Once a week he would don his purple sash, which was kept well hidden in the back of his closet behind several coat hangers of shirts and suits, properly stored so that none of his children would ever know that it was there and be tempted to play with it. Then he would hoof it the two blocks to the hall.

The phone rang one evening while dad was down at a meeting. After a brief conversation my mother turned to me and said there was an emergency. She sent me running down to the Masonic Hall for Dad.

Arriving at the hall door after a full sprint, I banged on the door as hard as I could. Moments later, a small door opened at the top of the main door. A man stuck his head out. Looking perturbed, he demanded to know my business and the reason for banging on the door so loudly.

His face changed after I got the words out. "Emergency . . . Dr. Moore needed."

"Okay, thank you," he said, and the little door was closed once more.

I started my walk home, pondering what secret business took place at those meetings. The small door got me thinking there must be some important, top secret stuff going on in that hall. Dad wouldn't say much.

On the next block up, on the left side of the road, was the fire hall followed by the police station, and then the village municipal office. Then came one of the most important buildings in the village: the large Sunderland Recreation Institute (SRI) Hall. A variety of activities took place there on its beautiful wood floor: dances, badminton, basketball, floor hockey, gymnastics, and boxing to name a few. Observers were treated to an aristocratic view from bleachers high on the northside wall. The school board must have had some kind of arrangement with the village because I can remember we had school house teams that sometimes played floor hockey down at the hall during lunchtime. I believe Cale was on the Goldenhawks team and, I'm not entirely confident of it, but I think I was with the Sputniks.

In the far-right corner of the hall was a very narrow, dark, and treacherous staircase that led down to the bowels of the building, where the boy's tiny changeroom was located. I didn't care for that room. It smelled.

VII

Long John Red Underwear

It was a dark, stormy night. Ha! I had no idea what the weather was like. It was night however, and my brother and I were absorbed in a drama playing out on our family's first colour television. We must have had the television for a while since neither of us called mum to report that our eyes were burning . . . as they had after watching the colour television too long on its first day in our house.

Some masked men had entered a big-city bank and were waving their weapons around while everyone hit the floor. Money was loaded into canvas backpacks. Suddenly sirens were heard. The police were on their way.

The robbers jumped into an elevator and headed to the roof of the building. Surely they were trapped. But one man pulled a rope and pully from his pack while another pulled a crossbow. An arrow, with rope attached was shot from the crossbow to an adjoining roof top. The rope was detached from the crossbow and secured to the bank rooftop. A man produced a bar which was somehow attached to the rope. It became clear that the robbers had a plan to escape, albeit a dangerous one.

This was getting exciting!

The leader of the robbers snugged his backpack, approached the edge of the roof, grabbed the bar, and rode the rope across perilously to the adjacent building's rooftop. Man! This was good. So dangerous. They were so high in the air. I'd never seen a building so high. Cal and I were transfixed.

Just then, Dad appeared in the doorway to the TV room.

"Hey, you guys, it's way past bedtime."

We recognized there was no amount of pleading that would allow us to continue watching.

"Off to bed, then," my father barked.

My brother trudged up the stairs leading to his bedroom while I walked across the hall to mine. My mind was still immersed in nervous excitement from the TV show as I changed into my long john red underwear. I don't know how I came to have that sleeping apparel, but on many a winter's night, I enjoyed their coziness.

As I drifted off to sleep, I kept thinking about the program.

Several hours later, I woke. At least, I say I woke, but it was to a kind of half-awake/half-asleep state. I just knew that I had to escape. The feeling was urgent. In a second I was standing on my bed, then walking to the end of it. I opened the very small window there, contorted my body to get through it . . . and jumped.

I woke the moment I landed—just like a cat. Well, I landed on two feet rather than four. The trip of three metres through the air to the ground had been quick.

I vividly remember looking across our yard to the telephone pole, from which light shone down from a large streetlight, illuminating and reflecting light off the loveliest fluffy falling snow that you can imagine. There was already about 10 centimetres of snow on the ground. It was a beautiful winter wonderland.

Suddenly, I realized my feet were very cold. I started lifting them into the air, one after another. Putting two and two together I concluded that my feet were cold because I was barefoot and standing in the aforementioned 10 centimetres of snow. Then the reality set in as to where I was. Standing in my yard, I was within visual range of the street. What if someone reported to my parents that they'd seen me outside in my underwear in the middle of the night?

I knew I had to get into the house, preferably without my father knowing anything about my adventure. *No problem*, I thought. I had never seen my parents lock the basement door. I ran around the side of the house, down the few steps to the door and tried it. What? It was locked. I then ran up the stairs to the veranda. I tried the main house door. Locked.

I stood there for a minute thinking about the locked doors. I guessed I'd never seen my parents lock the doors because they did that when they were turning in, well after we children had gone to bed.

I had to do something. I went to the kitchen window and tapped very quietly on it, hoping (okay, praying) that my brother would hear me and come down the stairs and let me in, without my father being none the wiser. Yes, I'd have to make a deal with him. He wouldn't tell my parents if I agreed to something or other. It would be worth it, though.

No response to my tapping. I tapped a little louder and waited. Nothing. I tapped louder yet. Suddenly, I could see light shining down the stairs.

A few moments later, I could see a rather large, hairy man, wearing a rumpled old housecoat. Guess who? To me the look on the man's face communicated something along the lines of, "Who dares to wake me in the middle of the night. I will eat you alive!"

I pulled back from the window and somehow found the courage to move my feet towards the door as I waited for my father to open it. I remember the shocked look on his face when he found me standing outside the door, shaking from the cold, in my long john red underwear, at about 4:30 a.m.

A burst of words shot out of my mouth. "Dad, you're not going to believe this: I was dreaming, and then I jumped out of my bedroom window and—"

I was cut off with three words.

"Get to bed!!!"

I recall moving pretty fast and yet as I rounded the corner to enter my bedroom I heard my father say, "We'll talk about this in the morning."

My heart sank. Grateful to soon be under my covers, I did have the thought that this one might be good for a record grounding.

I heard noise in the kitchen a few hours later and soon joined my brother and my father who were having breakfast.

Wanting to get things over with, I spoke. "Dad, can we talk about what happened last night?"

"Once your brother gets off to school we'll have a talk."

I had cornflakes for my, "last supper."

Soon, Cal was sent off to school and my father joined me at the kitchen table. I told him the whole story from A to Z. My father listened.

I ended with, "Dad, what will my punishment be?"

"Well," he paused for a moment and then continued, "I don't think you did that on purpose ... "

I waited.

". . . and so there will be no punishment. You can get your things and head off to school."

I couldn't believe it. I'm sure I was at the door with my things in seconds, just in case he changed his mind.

"Wait a minute," he spoke before I was out the door. "Of all my children, you are the one who seems to do some very, shall I say, INTERESTING things. I'm sure you will tell this story many times, to many people. Off you go."

What? My internal dialogue shouted. *I'm going to be telling people about jumping out of my bedroom window in the middle of the night, in my underwear?*

But he was right. Years later, I would tell the story to my classes when I was an elementary teacher, and sometimes when I visited classrooms as an elementary school counsellor. I'd usually end with, "So when you're having dinner tonight and one of your parents asks you what you talked about at school today . . . PLEASE don't say, "The school counsellor came to our classroom and talked about underwear!"

VIII

Each year, a week or two before Christmas Day, my father would scour the basement in search of his axe, which could be found just about anywhere depending on where one of his children had left it. It was time to get a Christmas tree!

We'd pile into the truck, which was destined to be parked somewhere along the road to the lake and trudge through the snow in search of a perfect Christmas tree. Those were the days when there were fewer of us and many more trees.

Inevitably, one of us hadn't worn lined winter boots, opting for the quick pull-on ubiquitous rubber boot. Unfortunately, it wasn't long before toes were frozen and the complaining would start. Dad would then do what he could to find a tree as quickly as he could. Often, a lovely tree could be found sticking out of the coal slag (black waste left from coal mining). My brother and I would get our turn to chop, and once the tree was down, we'd disappear into the tree's branches as we dragged it through the snow to the truck.

Those Douglas fir trees sure had a lot of pitch on them, which would inevitably be on us. What a sticky, sticky, fragrant resin it was. Indigenous people of the Northwest were known to use the resin for waterproofing canoes and tools. Supposedly, the resin also stimulates immunity against colds and boosts energy. The Indigenous people would make a tea out of the tree tips or needles.

We would return home with pitch on our skin and clothes. Mum would most often be waiting with a bar of butter, her go-to pitch remover, which she would slather on our skin and our clothes. Yuck!

Now you may have noticed my spelling of "Mum." My mother preferred that spelling; I guess it had to do with her Scottish roots, of which she was inordinately proud and always curious to explore. She loved things to do with the old country. In her later years. she'd go crazy over Mel Gibson's, *Braveheart*. One time my brother-in-law and I were over at her home in Alston. She was watching her VCR tape of *Braveheart* yet again. When it came to a scene where a character started speaking in a language other than English, my mother jumped up, threw her hand up into the air and shouted out, "Gaelic!"

To which I corrected, "Actually . . . Mum, that's French." Which it was.

Mum's connection to Scotland was direct. Her mother had been a Scottish lassie—in fact, a "Burns."

I discovered years later that many of my distant cousins in Scotland named their sons "Robbie" in honour of that great Scottish rascal poet Robbie Burns. On one trip to Scotland, I was to meet a cousin, Robbie Burns, at a pub in Aberdeen, the "Granite City." I was having no luck finding him despite searching in the pub and the square just outside of it. Finally, I walked up to a red-faced Scot who had a prominent roadmap of veins on his good-sized nose. I put the question to him, "I'm looking for my cousin, Robbie Burns; do you know him?"

"Hell man," he replied without hesitation, pointing a finger across the street: "You're way too late. There's a statue of him over there!"

. . .

Christmas 2020

My wife and I have just arrived home from dinner at my daughter's, 56 years on from Christmas 1964. My daughter is married to a good man. They have three sons: a four-year-old and a two-year-old, both afflicted with the excitement of Christmas; and a three-month-old who does not yet know the wonder of the season (by far he is the easiest to buy for. I could screw up and buy him a dog toy and he wouldn't know the difference).

Somehow, I couldn't resist approaching their Christmas tree several times during the visit, bending to smell that smell of a freshly cut Douglas fir. Do you know that smell?

And I hoped not to use my eyes during the visit but to see things unfold through the eyes of my grandchildren. That was not easy to accomplish but fleeting moments reward with the wonderment of Christmas. That was the best gift.

As we drove into our Clifton neighbourhood, which was adorned with festive lights, I found myself feeling the melancholy, which has visited in recent Christmas times. But Christmas 1964 and every Christmas of my childhood was far from melancholic.

. . .

Christmas 1964

It took a number of years to figger it out, but I eventually did. We would be spoiled on Christmas morning, even if we hadn't been quite that good. Most often, we would find a toy under the tree that we'd asked our parents for a hundred times or more. And to be doubly sure, we'd cover our bases by sending letters to Santa.

We got our Christmas present ideas from two sources in those days. The first was the thick and heavy Eaton's catalogue that would come in the mail, strategically sent to homes sometime in November. There were pages upon pages of toys to consider. The second source of ideas was the advertising on television, which would be taken up a notch as Christmas neared.

Each year, I would wake my brother in the middle of the night. We would walk, tippytoed, down the hallway, being particularly quiet as we passed my parent's bedroom door, and begin our descent of the stairs. Calvin wasn't as light on his feet as I was; most often a foot of his, placed a tad heavy on a stair, was enough to rouse my mother who would hurry us back to bed with our mission incomplete.

Eventually, I determined that the best chance of success dictated a solo mission. For years, my mother would tell the story of the time she woke with the sense she should check the top of the stairs for unauthorized persons. Arriving at the top of the stairs, she found no children but she could see a dim light shining downstairs. She will tell the story from here.

Once I was almost at the bottom of the stairs I could determine the light was coming from the TV room where Dad and I had been a few hours earlier, placing gifts around the Christmas tree. Entering the room, I found Stuey, standing frozen, with eyes big and round, staring at the gifts.

"Stu, get back to bed!"

"Just let me have one look," he replied. And sure enough in a few seconds he pivoted and quietly retreated upstairs.

. . .

I was over the top on Christmas day 1964 because Santa got me a Johnny Seven. I would no longer be outgunned in combat. Most of my friends had a tommy gun. I had that and much more!

The Johnny Seven was a multi-function weapon and became a huge selling toy among boys. It had a grenade launcher, repeating rifle, automatic pistol, anti-tank rocket, anti-bunker missile, tommy gun, and armour-piercing shell.

I had seen the television advertisement a million times and pleaded with my parents to get it for me for Christmas. Of course, not everyone thought it was the best toy out there for children. There's a story out there that Captain Kangaroo (Bob Keeshan) refused to allow adverts for Johnny Seven to be shown when his TV program was broadcast.

The brave young soldier wielded his weapon with a confidence beyond his years. Switching effortlessly between the modes his great gun offered, within minutes he took out a tank, an armoured vehicle, and send several enemy troops scurrying for cover. He knew another commendation would be recommended by his sergeant. But, he fought for country not for individual recognition.

Suddenly his peripheral vision caught a solitary enemy coming into range. This German soldier was different. Smaller, much nimbler, despite carrying a whole kit. Likely sent in first, perhaps as a forward scout.

The young soldier calmed himself. This would be a long-range shot requiring finesse. Setting his weapon to single shot, he waited patiently for the German to come into range. As he waited he became aware of drips of sweat on his forehead . . . he knew this happened when there was a lot on the line.

The German was just within range now. Before the soldier could squeeze the trigger, he spotted a German general, of all things, on the battlefield.

The general spoke, "Stu, you've had your fun now. I don't want you shooting your little sister any more today. How about putting the toy away for a while?"

. . .

My mum and her sister, Jean, would take turns each Christmas cooking a wonderful turkey dinner. Auntie Jean and Uncle Gordie lived in Clifton and had two children, Greig and Gavin. Greig was a year younger than Lena. Gavin was another three years younger than Greig.

We kids would run around in our house while the final touches were being put on dinner. Usually, we would manage to get some of the Christmas tree needles stuck in our sock feet. There was often a trail of them throughout the house by the time we were called for dinner.

Each year, there would be mouth-watering turkey, mashed potatoes, Brussels Sprouts, gravy (aka, liquid gold), and cranberry sauce, served on our finest china. I remember the special little crystal salt and pepper shakers that were brought out for the occasion. They'd crisscross the table many times during the course of the meal.

My father preferred dark turkey meat. I thought he had strange tastes when it came to food. For Dad, Mr. Maffetti actually saved bananas that had gone soft and black! The explanation being that Dad had grown up on a farm near Minnedosa, Manitoba, so most often when he got his hands on a banana, it was on its way out, and so he developed a taste for it. Another prairie-people favourite that sometimes made its way to the table was mashed turnips. We children defended our plates as best we could from Mum dropping a scoop of that orange mush onto them.

Each year, there would be the usual challenge to get little Gavin to eat something. Various strategies were employed to no avail. I figgered the kid was going to be a little runt his whole life because of his eating habits, but low and behold he turned out to be of average height. I distinctly remember Uncle Gordie being very concerned.

Lena would somehow manage to procure and consume the majority of the turkey stuffing, much to everyone's chagrin. There hasn't been a Christmas dinner over the past 55 or so years in which I've failed to share the story, and if Lena happened to be present, suggested to those around the table the need to keep an eye on her.

We would all get a sampling of whatever kind of Baby Duck sparkling wine was up for grabs. My parents were definitely not wine connoisseurs. I didn't know it at the time, but in its day Baby Duck was the best-selling Canadian wine. Apparently, the manufacturer tried to get it to catch on in Britain but it was a flop. The *London Sunday Times'* review probably didn't help: "The drink is purple, sparkling stuff that tastes like black current wine gum dissolved in a glass of Andrews Liver Salt. Served extremely cold — preferably on a stick—you might be amused by its presumption."

It seemed that the one thing that little Gavin would consume was the wine! There was the one Christmas dinner where Cal and I slipped Gavin the wine from our glasses. It made for an entertaining evening.

Oh, and the omnipresent shortbread at Christmas time. My mother's shortbread were frequently quite brown on the bottom, the consequence of a cook who had many things to do. But how we loved them. Once, a very good friend of my mother's commented that the shortbread were burned. My Mum responded matter- of-factly: "The kids like them that way."

. . .

Back in the day, Mandarin oranges (we called them Japanese oranges) were absent from the fruit and vegetables aisle at Clifton's Safeway until just before Christmas. They disappeared shortly after. You just couldn't get them at other times of the year. They were a real treat, and I had no idea how their presence on our kitchen counter could define those that had more versus those that had less.

63

My family was better off than most of my friends' families. I didn't realize it all at once. I knew that our house was bigger; friends had commented on it. I never heard my parents argue about lack of money. We went on holidays, sometimes in an airplane, to places far from Sunderland. Kids at school told me that doctors got paid a lot of money. Thankfully, we weren't bullied about it very often.

I recall a time when Calvin's classmate, Andy Stevens, came over to our house to play with Cal. They disappeared upstairs to Cal's room. I'm sure Cal would have shown him the models he'd constructed from kits and then painted: The Wolfman, Frankenstein, and my favourite, The Creature from the Black Lagoon. He'd done a really good job on them.

In a while they were downstairs watching TV. Cal left to grab a couple of Japanese oranges from the kitchen. One for himself and one for Andy. And then there were more trips to get more oranges. Andy started following Cal to the kitchen and was amazed to see an entire box of Japanese oranges, seemingly available for kids to help themselves to whenever they wanted.

The next day at school, Andy was spreading it around the playground that the Moore kids could eat treats like Japanese oranges whenever they wanted.

I can't recall the details of the conversation Mum had with us that night. I just recall the sense that Mum was embarrassed and Cal was ashamed.

. . .

It hadn't been a difficult decision, that one Christmas time evening when I'd decided to run away. I don't recollect my issue with the Moore family at the time, but I remember the feeling that I'd "had enough of them." I rolled up a few things in a towel and attached it to the end of my broken hockey stick. The stick that Billy Montrose had made for me out of a couple of broken ones. The glue hadn't held. The first time I took a shot, the blade broke right off. I'd leaned the shaft in a corner of the basement, knowing I'd find a use for it sooner or later.

I knew it was necessary to have a bundle on the end of a stick when one wanted to run away. I'd seen it on Walt Disney's *Huckleberry Finn*. Out the front door I went. There were about 30 centimetres of snow on the ground. I walked down the first set of steps from the house. It was snowing, and a nasty wind blew, which made it quite miserable out. I walked down to the next set of stairs and stepped down almost to the bottom of them. There I laid in the snow that covered the side of the steps. It was cold. I swallowed the first few snowflakes that landed near my mouth. I closed my eyes and pondered my future as a free man.

Twenty minutes or so later, I heard the front door to the house open.

"Stuey, it's getting pretty cold out there now," my mum said. "You'd better come in."

"I'm running away!" I shouted.

"You have run away," she said. "You did it! I'm going to make some hot chocolate now."

A hug and a cup of chocolate was what I needed. And those are what I got.

IX

Our house had been very grand in its day. A number of years ago, the village council recognized it as a heritage home. There is a plaque on a post in front of the house that reads:

> *"The Home was built in 1910 by the Canadian Bank of Commerce for Daniel Lorne White, the new Bank Manager. In 1917 the Bank sold the property to Canadian Collieries Dunsmuir Ltd. And the new mine Superintendent, C. Patterson, moved in. The Pattersons held garden parties and teas, making the home a social centre in the 1920's. From 1931 to 1959 various mining officials resided in the home until 1959, when Dr. C.B. Moore and his wife Margaret, purchased the home. They resided here until the late 1970's. The home is a side-gabled, one and a half storey Craftsman Bungalow prefabricated, and brought by train from Collection Bay. The grounds were extensive, and terraced with several sets of stairs leading to a large circular driveway."*

The home was very large and well-equipped for its time. There were three bedrooms on the top floor, all with large closets. The bedroom my brother and I shared until we were about age 11 and 10 respectively, when irreconcilable differences prompted my parents to move me down to the main floor, had its own porcelain sink. I imagine many distinguished guests to the home in the early 1900s found it a special convenience. Come to think of it, my brother and I did, too, as we used it successfully as a urinal for a while before we were found out by the landlord at the time: our father.

Just outside this bedroom was a linen closet that housed an almost two-metre-high cardboard figure belonging to my brother. Many a time a family member, entering that closet to retrieve a blanket or a sheet, had the bejesus scared out of them, because upon flipping the light switch, front and centre was FRANKENSTEIN!

Actually, there was something even scarier than Frankenstein in that room, although I doubt my siblings knew about it. Snooping around in there one day, I came across one of my dad's medical texts, stuck away in a drawer in the corner. There were pictures that terrified me . . . . various deformities and skin conditions.

Next to the linen closet was a bathroom, whose window provided convenient access to part of the home's roof, should one be up for an adventure. That section of the roof was risky, however, since it was in full view of someone returning home from work, driving down Hospital Hill in his red VW Beetle. And it didn't help that one child that called the house home had a tendency to impulsive urges, which overrode his ability to learn from the negative consequences he'd received the last time he was caught.

At the opposite end of the top floor to Cal's bedroom was my parent's bedroom. My sister Lena's bedroom was next to my parent's. I have memory of a small phonograph with a well-worn Bobby Sherman record ready to be played in Lena's room. There is a time capsule that my mother packed away in a closet that was on the right side of the room (my parents had the closet door drywalled over and wallpapered). I donated my cap gun six shooter.

I fully expect to be invited by the present owner of the home to a special ceremonial opening of the time capsule once I am a world-famous author.

Down the stairs to the main floor revealed a spacious living area for its day. Laundry room, kitchen, dining room, living room, "piano" room, TV room, bathroom, and my bedroom.

The laundry room was really just a little alcove off the back door entrance to the house. There was just room for a washer machine and dryer. Hmmm. Flashback to when, as six-year-olds, Jack Walston and I put Calvin's cat, Colourful, into the dryer. Luckily, Mum heard the thump and ran to terminate our experiment.

We spent the majority of our time in the TV room. I recall as clear as day the news of President Kennedy's assassination on November 22, 1963. I was seven years old. I ran to the kitchen and told Mum that I was so proud of being an American. I was disappointed that I had to settle for being a Canadian.

There were two popular spots in the TV room that Lena, Calvin, and I competed for. The first was the loveseat, which was the ideal location to stretch out and watch television. There should have been a plaque on the front of it, identifying that this was the location where my exhausted mother had fallen asleep several years earlier after chasing her two toddlers, only to be awoken by a sharp pain in her nose and discovering that the pain was from me shoving my little finger up as far as I could.

The second prime spot was on the carpeted floor by a vent. It was highly treasured in the winter. Warm arm would exit the vent, coming from the oil forced-air furnace. Such a pleasure to remove wet socks and place frozen feet on the vent.

There was a time when battle royals would break out to determine who had what spot, but we sorted it out. True, it wasn't quite the same as Roosevelt, Churchill, and Stalin meeting to discuss the postwar reorganization of Germany and Europe, but we three kids gave serious consideration to developing an agreement that would reduce conflict, if not in all jurisdictions . . . at least in our TV room.

If, "Save my spot!" was shouted before vacating the room for a short period of time, say, to use the facilities, one could return to the TV room assured that the spot had been reserved for them.

· · ·

Cal and I were only 11 months apart, so there was a fair amount of overlap in our development. I say, "Sure, sure," to the thought my brother would say, "Yeah, maybe early on, but then you stopped developing as a teenager."

Mum was kept pretty busy with two boys going through potty training at more or less the same time. She'd plunk whoever had to "go" down on the toilet seat and leave him to do his business. I guess at one juncture Mum had confidence that we could handle the first part of the process, actually staying seated unsupervised, but she must have been less sure about our ability to clean up, since she trained us to say loudly, "DONE!" when we were . . . done. She would then come and give a wipe.

I think the system worked quite well, and the memory of it had more or less disappeared, but little did I know that Calvin was going to remind the entire family of it years later. It must have been during a break from university when Cal had come home from SFU, and me from UVIC. The whole family had just finished a great meal. I think we even had some wine on that particular occasion. Anyway, Cal excused himself from the table and disappeared down the hallway, I assumed to retire to the bathroom. A few minutes later, my 20-something-year-old brother shouted out, "DONE!" We had quite a laugh over that blast from the past.

· · ·

Like many a great invention, it is simple in nature and yet profound in its potential to advance the human race. It's a toilet seat lifter or lowerer. Okay, perhaps I need to work on the device's name. I can't say for certain when the idea first came to me. I'd heard, "Put the toilet seat down when you're finished," as I'm sure many a boy has heard, many a time. Think about it. A universal device made of plastic and springs that can be set to lower or raise a toilet seat automatically. There's money in it. I know it. If this best-selling book gig doesn't work out, I might go there. In the meantime, consider it my gift to you if you want to pursue a patent and make your fortune.

I had another great idea but unfortunately time has eroded its potential. Think of a pair of black framed glasses without lenses. On one of the glasses' arms is a beer bottle opener . . . an essential in pre-screw top bottle days. On the other arm are three half circles of metal where three cigarettes could be inserted so that they stood straight up, easily accessible. I called this invention: "Drinking Glasses." I know. I should have moved on its way back then. I know how the inventor of the eight-track player feels.

. . .

When Cal and I were around four and three years old, respectively, we had a couple of friends, the Clark brothers, who were the same age as us. They lived close by. In fact, if you walked about 20 metres up Hospital Hill and cut down the alley to the right, theirs was the second house. Being friends with them must have worked out well for both mothers. They could keep a close eye on us four if we played in the alley or on the stumps near our garage, which was our favourite place to goof around and get dirty.

One day, Dad had taken Cal and I somewhere . . . not sure where. Most likely, Mum had told Dad, "Just take them away for a while . . . anywhere."

Mum was having a wonderful nap on the loveseat in the TV room when she woke, sensing she wasn't alone in the house. Who could it be? It was too early for us to have returned. Dad knew better than to bring us back that quick.

Mum walked out of the TV room, into the hallway, startled when she heard a noise coming from the direction of the bathroom. Turning, she looked past the wide-open bathroom door to see one of the Clark boys sitting on the toilet with his short pants down around his ankles.

"What are you doing in here?" she asked, meaning what are you doing in *our* house?

"Going poo," replied the Clark boy, forever sealing his fate in Moore folklore.

• • •

From the main living floor of our house there was another set of stairs leading down to the very large basement. It was mostly open in the centre but had rooms: a wine cellar room, storage room, tool room, and coal room. The coal room was, as you might predict, dirty and black. It had a large sled door covered with tin sheeting that would have been dropped open when coal was shovelled in from the outside. But that was before my time.

My father had the coal room converted to a workshop with wall attached work benches around the periphery. There were a few manual saws, hammers, screwdrivers, and a vise.

I can't recall any masterful woodwork projects being constructed in the room by . . . anyone. I know that I found it to be a convenient place if I ever had anything that I needed to smash up. I was a master at deconstruction projects.

My brother did a temporary conversion to the workshop one spring. He turned it into a horror house. And I mean a horror house! For a five-cent entrance fee, a neighbourhood kid could be traumatized. I know, because my job was to stand at the stairs leading to the basement and collect the entrance fee from those naïve children. Many entered with smiles on their faces and in a state of excited anticipation, only to come bolting out of the basement minutes later, grateful to be out in the light of day.

There was the standard bowl of eyeballs (grapes), a brain (was it broccoli or cauliflower?), and creepy Halloween music set the tone. But Cal's star exhibit set him apart from any potential neighbourhood competition. His horror house had a real human skeleton. The bones were wired into place, and the bottom jaw could be moved since it had springs holding it to the upper mandible. Most of the teeth were still there. I don't think Dad knew that the skeleton he had agreed to store for the St. John's Ambulance Society was the real show-stopper in Cal's horror house.

X

Dinner was usually planned for six o'clock, although many times my dad didn't arrive home from work in time to eat with us. And sometimes he'd get called out in the evening and so there were days we didn't get a lot of time with him.

I can see him as clear as day, entering the exterior door at the kitchen. I was there in a flash. I put my sock feet on his shoes. I wrapped my arms around his waist. He danced me around the room.

And then he said, "Stuey, I'm tired. I have to rest now," and so off I'd go to the TV room to join my siblings. A few minutes later, while Mum was putting the finishing touches on dinner, we could hear my father playing the piano. There's a hesitation in his playing every few moments, something my piano teacher would want addressed. But, my father has never had a lesson.

I don't know why but one day I took my pocketknife and carved my initials, S. M. in the upper-right corner of the piano. I suppose Sigmund Freud would have a theory.

Shortly after, Dad came home from work that day and had retreated to the living room for some relaxation. We heard the shout: "STUART!" Boy, did I ever get it for that one.

The next day when Dad sought solace at the piano, right below my initials, carved larger and more primary-like were the initials,

L. M. We heard the shout, "LENA!" And Lena got in trouble. And then, I got in more trouble . . . because Lena had copied me.

Of course, younger siblings learn from watching their older siblings (sometimes that learning isn't that helpful, for example carving one's initials into a piano in response to an older brother's modelling).

From time to time, Lena had seen either Calvin or me run into a store to get a treat for everyone. It came for the time for her to give it a try. Mum had pulled the car over at a small store in Clifton, just off Sunderland Road. She coaxed Lena to ask each of us in turn what we would like for a snack. Cal wanted Old Dutch potato chips, I wanted a Pepsi, and Mum wanted a grape pop, which she held allegiance to forever. Lena stuck out her little hand and Mum placed a five-dollar bill into it. Off she went, super excited to be a grown-up girl.

I saw the smile on her face as she exited the store. She climbed into the car holding tightly onto the brown paper bag that the clerk had filled with her purchases. She reached into the bag and began the ceremony.

"Mum, here is your grape pop. Stu, here is your Pepsi. Here's my chocolate bar. Calvin, here is your Old Dutch." She passed the container of Old Dutch kitchen cleanser to Cal.

. . .

As an alternative to unwinding by playing a few minutes of piano, Dad would sometimes work on the day's *Vancouver Sun* newspaper crossword puzzle. There he is now, in my mind. Sitting at the head of the sixties Arborite topped kitchen table, pencil in hand. He was very good at them.

It would have been helpful, I'm sure, if I'd developed an interest in them. Perhaps it would have limited some potential negative reviews of this writing endeavour due to my limited vocabulary.

When I'm discouraged, I can imagine my book reviews: "Too many two-syllable words" . . . "Firestarter" . . . or the review in the *London Times*: "Absolute gobshite." My own brother-in-law has requested that his copy of the book be printed in two-ply paper! Har de har har! I don't suppose he'll ever read it anyway since I have no plans to publish a picture book version.

Oh well, I shall press on!

. . .

Mum used to tell the story about a morning when I was being particularly annoying to everyone (there was only that one morning). She suggested maybe I could do a job, I guess with the hope if I was busy doing something, everyone would get a break from my incessant attention-seeking. I loved the idea of a job, especially if it was a paying job. After haggling for a period of time, we agreed that I would make everyone's bed for 5 cents each. According to Mum, I disappeared instantly. She was impressed, both with her plan and my initiative. She was just settling into a comfortable peacefulness brought about by my absence, when I suddenly appeared and asked for payment.

"The beds aren't done already, are they? she queried.

"They're all done, Mum," I answered proudly.

"Well, let's have a look, then," she said suspiciously.

The way Mum told it, we first went to Lena's bedroom. The bed didn't look too bad. Then we went to Cal's and my room. The quality of job there was poor, borderline acceptable. Finally, we went to my parents' bedroom.

"Why, this bed doesn't even look like you made it," she declared.

To which I replied, "I didn't. I gave Lena a penny to make it."

Lena was a pretty good little sister, as far as little sisters go. All right! I admit it! I probably traumatized her to an extent, but at the time I was under the impression that it was part of an older brother's job description.

I remember the noise and the broken glass everywhere when Lena smashed the textured window at the top of the bathroom door. I wish I could just leave it at that but if this is confession time, I admit I pestered her to the point that she grabbed whatever was close by to throw at me. I ducked. Do you know that those Barbie Dolls from the sixties can actually shatter a window if thrown with sufficient velocity?

And while I'm on the topic of Lena . . . I always felt like mum had extra sensory perception or some kind of special power that would tell her what we boys were up to. I wonder if Lena wasn't Mum's secret weapon, revealing to her whatever nonsense we were up to or planning to do. Confess, Lena!

I can still conjure up negative feelings towards Lena by remembering my beloved six-finger baseball mitt. It was my pride and joy. I'd taken it from a stiff cowhide leather glove when I first purchased it from a Clifton sports store, to a soft, flexible extension of my baseball player's soul, by using the time-tested combination of repeatedly throwing a ball into the pocket and using copious amounts of spit.

It broke my heart when it disappeared forever. Lena had borrowed it (WITHOUT PERMISSION) for a girls' softball practice and left it behind at the top field.

My good buddy, Foo, will recall that it was that very mitt that I used to make, "The Catch."

Our boys' softball team was in Alston, aiming to show those Alston hicks (yeah, they were the hicks . . . we lived in a huge urban area of 1,500 people) how the game was meant to be played. We had a good team, anchored by our phenomenal pitcher, Stuckle. Boy, that guy could throw a softball. Big windup, intimidating speed. I didn't like to face him, even in practice. I used to get a kick out of looking at the faces of opposing team batters after Stuckle blew a pitch by them.

I was by no means a superstar. On that particular day, I was playing left field. An Alston hitter smacked a high fly to right centre field. I don't know why, but I took off for it at full speed, soon passing the centre fielder and almost running into the right fielder. My mitt was pushed towards the heavens by my left arm. The ball landed smack into my six-finger glove. The team cheered.

Many a time, Foo would tell that story over the years. I prefer that one to the story he tells of my prowess as a soccer defence-man. Foo was our goaltender so he got to witness my work in front of him all the time. When an opposing player was closing in on the net, I'd resort to my go-to move: the shin hack. A fair number of my adversaries ended up rolling around on the turf, clutching their sore shins. Yes, I am claiming that I was largely responsible for keeping Foo's goals against average down. I think deep down Foo knows that.

. . .

Foo had a younger brother, Barry, aka, "Little Foo."

There he is in my mind's eye. He's playing outside his family's store, Cheung's Grocery. He's a cute little shrimp, running around with his little stick legs protruding from short pants. I'm waiting for Jack Walston, who is riding his bike up from his house, which is way down by the park.

"I'll meet you at Cheung's," Jack had said over the phone. "Your place is too far and most of the ride is uphill." I had agreed to his terms. It sounded fair.

"Hey . . . Little Foo, can you get me a bag of chips?" I said without thinking.

Little Foo sprinted around the corner into the store. Seconds later, he returned with a bag of Old Dutch potato chips. I couldn't believe it. I tore open the bag and offered him a chip. Before Jack arrived, I saw Mum's red Ford Falcon convertible approaching. My mum pulled over.

"Where did you get the bag of chips?" she asked.

How did she always know?

It must have been a couple of years after the chips incident when I'd gone to Foo's house to see if he wanted to play. He wasn't around. Somehow, Little Foo ended up being my playmate that afternoon.

We eventually got way up to the Number Five Mine road. There was an area there where the village workers had just done some blasting. There were huge slabs of granite spread around. It looked like a scene from an alien planet I'd seen on *Star Trek*.

Little Foo and I split up. He hid behind a splintered rock. I hid behind another. We were on the go. I was Captain Kirk. I picked up a walnut-sized rock and bounced it off the big slab I believed Little Foo was hiding behind. I fired more. I was on an alien planet engaged in a solo battle with another life form. There was a lot at stake.

Little Foo stuck his head up from behind the slab just as a rock arrived. He let out a loud wail. He was cut above one eyebrow.

What had I done? I ran towards him. He was bleeding profusely. I didn't know what to do. Then I remembered something I'd seen on TV. I removed my white T-shirt and pressed it against his head. We started the walk back to Little Foo's house. He sobbed most of the way. My T-shirt was half full of Little Foo's blood.

. . .

July 1988

I was summoned from my graduate program counselling class at the University of British Columbia by a clerk. She told me the acting dean of the Department of Counselling Psychology would like to meet me in his office.

The dean asked me what my plans were. I told him I was anxious to complete my master's degree and seek employment as a school counsellor. He asked if I'd thought about continuing on to work on a doctorate.

Me? Have the letters "DR" before my name? I told him no. He said that he'd heard about me from my graduate program supervisor. If I was interested, he would sponsor me in the doctorate program.

It was surreal. What was happening? I think he'd made a mistake. Did he really know who I am?

XI

*"Until one has loved an animal, a part of one's soul
remains unawakened."*

—*Anatole France*

Our house at 601 First Street was also home to a number of pets.
The first on the scene was Pixie, my dog. I have so many fond
memories of her. Mum said she was a mix. I was stuck on that
one. At the time, I only knew of a pancake mix. She was mid-sized,
brown and yellowish orange, had a face narrower than a spaniel,
and had that thickness of coat that prompted my mother to give a
shaving to every summer. She was my first love, and I believe her
omnipresent quality of tolerance was something I gravitated to in
future love relationships. Ears and tail could be pulled, horseback
rides attempted . . . she just hung in there. Although in her later
years, she spent more and more time in her "safe" place, sleeping
behind the loveseat. Let me clarify. I don't mean to suggest that I
pull my wife's ears, that she has a tail, or that she is pressured into
giving me horseback rides. And, so far, please note, my wife has
not felt the need to hide behind a loveseat.

"Colourful" was Calvin's cat. She was the lady of the manor. A
beautiful calico. Elegant. Soft spoken, like her master. When she

aristocratically strode into a room, everyone's attention turned towards her. Cal would frequently walk around the house with Colourful hanging over his shoulder.

And now, Ladies and Gentlemen . . . KOBBY TIKI! Kobby was Lena's pug. He came onto the scene a little later than Pixie and Colourful. Where to begin!? He was our "You know every family has one."

I don't think he was ever properly house-trained and I suspect it was because Kobby didn't want to be properly house-trained. He was . . . independently minded. That's what Dad used to say. One of his favourite targets was a corner leg of my bed. Oh, and that corner of the bedspread too, since he tended to be very thorough when he set about to his work. A secondary target was the aluminum garbage can just outside the kitchen door on the veranda. I mean, why bother to go to the trouble of hopping down the veranda stairs to the lawn. Do you know in the winter it would freeze to an amber glaze?

Kobby was known to be determinedly vengeful. I know this for a fact. Do you know how much effort it takes for 10-centimetre-long legs to carry a dog's body up a large number of stairs so that the patriarch's bedroom can be accessed? And the effort to jump up onto my father's bed? We were all summoned to view the poor excuse for a mini-Snickers chocolate bar that was left perfectly centred on the bed, as if its location had been mathematically calculated. Kobby!

And Kobby somehow convinced Calvin's classmate and friend Gumper that Gumper had successfully taught Kobby a trick: how to hump Gumper's leg on demand. Kobby!

The dog was crazy. One time I saw him in our yard chewing on a plastic pea shooter. I know he ate it, because later I saw it come out of his other end in pieces. Kobby!

But, *le dernier grand cours*, was the "rope and ball." Somehow Kobby found, and ate, a piece of regular white string, the kind of string that might be used to wrap up a parcel for mailing. We know he ate it because he came back into the house after a short outside visit with about three inches of string hanging outside of his, um, distal orifice. But Kobby was no ordinary talent. At the end of the string was a perfectly round ball of poo, which swung back and forth as he chased we children around the TV room.

Our screams, and there were many, as we competed for refuge on top of the couch, were soon responded to by my mother, who entered the room, once again exhibiting a facial expression that belied her further astonishment of what this dog was capable of.

Lena wouldn't do it, Calvin wouldn't do it, and I sure as heck wasn't going to do it. My mum got some toilet paper and slowly and carefully extracted "it" from Kobby's rear porthole. Truly, Kobby was the "gift that kept on giving," before the expression was even coined. Kobby!

. . .

Kobby wasn't the only interesting dog in the neighbourhood. There was Spike, the Randle's dog. He was some kind of hound dog/hunter mix, with brown and white patches on the top, white with brown "freckles" all over his tummy and his private parts. Whenever I went over to visit my buddy Chunk Randle at his place, Spike was always lying fast asleep on their dirt driveway, often with his tongue hanging out. I couldn't figger it out. He was unlike any other dog I'd ever known. He wouldn't bark when anyone entered the yard. He would show absolutely no interest whenever I tried to throw a stick for him. He just slept.

I eventually solved the mystery. On a beautiful sunny day, I was riding my bike all around town. First I saw Spike down by the park with a female dog friend doing what dogs do (not fighting, in this case). Later, I saw him with another female dog friend over in another part of the village. And finally, when I reported these events to Chunk when I was almost home, he said he'd seen Spike so engaged with his neighbour's dog that very morning. Spike!

. . .

Dad told my brother and I that of all the animals he grew up with on the farm back in Manitoba, he loved horses the most. So it wasn't a shock, and we were certainly excited, when we were told that he'd bought a horse. Goldie was an old nag. She must have had some draft horse blood because she was so wide across her back that when I rode double behind my dad my legs would stick straight out. And you had to be careful around her because if one of her huge hooves came down on your foot you'd have a broken foot; at least that's what Dad used to say. I believed him.

It wasn't long after we got Goldie that Dad purchased two ponies: Daffy, and her filly, Dilly. And shortly thereafter Daffy gave birth to Barney.

I was trying to figure out how horses had babies. Dad explained that the male horse plants his seed in the female horse. I accepted that. I'd seen one horse chasing after another and biting it on the neck. I figgered that's how they planted their seed. It seemed logical.

We kids were the envy of our friends for having a pony each, and there were many years of fun down at the barn. However, as the number of horses increased over time, my interest decreased. There was so much work associated with horses.

In the beginning when we had few horses and Cal and I were young, my parents managed the chores and we were mostly exempt. But as we gained more horses and Cal and I got older, there were lots of chores. It was certainly not all fun and games. You couldn't spend all of your day down at the barn playing tag on horseback or throwing balls of manure at one another.

The first barn that was built didn't have running water or lights. We had to transport each horse's water bucket outside, where there was one tap a short distance away. Once those heavy-duty black rubber buckets were full of water they were heavy. For sources of light, particularly on dark winter mornings or early evenings, Dad would light kerosene lanterns and hang them in a few strategic places in the barn. Then there was feeding the horses: grain and hay, twice a day. We'd get grain from Buckerfields in Clifton. It came in 23-kilogram bags. We'd lug them down to the basement in our home. Dad was concerned about rats in the barn, so just a few bags were kept there inside a big wooden feed box that the rats couldn't get into.

Dad had a number of different sources for hay. Sometimes we'd get a few bales from Buckerfields. Most often, if he could find good local hay we'd pick it up right from the farm. From trial and error, error being a bale or two falling off the back of our truck, Dad learned precisely how many bales we could take and how they had to be arranged. Sometimes a huge truck and trailer would stop by with those damn heavy alfalfa bales. They were dense and held together by two wires rather than the standard binder twine. The bales would end up in the hayloft, stacked by yours truly when I was strong enough. I hated going up there. I'd sneeze like crazy. It seemed I'd produce an endless amount of snot. Lena called me "Snod," a combo nickname, based on my abundance of snot and that she perceived I always acted like I was God. I had to credit the kid for her creativity. But thankfully the name didn't stick.

The horses would have to be brushed, and they required regular exercise. I know, it sounds like I'm complaining about horseback riding. You're thinking what kid wouldn't love the opportunity to ride. But when there were a lot of horses to exercise . . . it was WORK.

Then there was the hardest chore of all: cleaning out the barn. At one point, we had about 10 horses in the barn. It was about then that the novelty of equine companionship started to wear off. Did you know that I am ambidextrous with a shovel? Dragging manure out from underneath and behind a horse in a stall will help you develop that. I'd pull the manure out of each stall first, creating a long line of manure to be thrown out a window at the end of the barn. I might have been on the skinny side at the time, but I got strong.

It wasn't long before there was a huge pile of steaming manure outside the barn window. At first, we'd shovel it into wheelbarrows and move it to another part of the barnyard. In other words: more labour. Once our new pile got too big, Dad advertised manure for sale in the local paper. It was a prized fertilizer.

If I happened to be around, I'd help the manure buyer shovel it into his trailer or truck bed.

As more horses were added to the stable, Dad realized we needed a tractor. Actually I think he also realized we needed a bigger barn, which he eventually had built.

The tractor cut down on labour. With its front-end loader, we could transport the outside manure pile over to another field and efficiently load manure for any purchaser. And, of course, there were many other uses for the tractor.

I'd sometimes take the tractor for a bomb on a trail that ran from the barn right up to an area of houses in Sunderland. Why? I don't know. It certainly didn't reward with the type of shifting that a car did. Mind you, top speed was adequate for the rough trail.

On a November day, I took it up the trail. It had been raining for days. There was land cleared next to the first houses I encountered. I guessed they were building new houses there. Anyway, I thought what a cool place to take the tractor. I was handy at getting a tractor unstuck by using the front loader, but in this case it was hopeless since the rear wheels sunk in the mud all the way down to the axles. I had no choice. I had to walk home and ask for Dad's help.

His reaction to my plight was, "It's okay. Sometimes this sort of thing happens. Let's jump in the car and I'll show you how to get it unstuck."

He drove down to the barn. "Where is it?" Dad asked as he scanned the barnyard and the field next to it for the colour orange.

"It's a little down the trail," I said.

"Down the trail," he repeated, sounding a little concerned.

Down the trail we drove. Dad's face got redder and redder. Finally, we got to Sunderland. He was not pleased. I've got to give it to him, though. He was better with that front-end loader than I was. He got the tractor out and positioned it on the trail for me to drive back to the barnyard. Then he got into his car with muddy pants up to his knees. He didn't have to say anything. I knew.

. . .

For some crazy reason, Apache Charlie moved his body towards the corner of the tin barn . . . just as I was throwing my leg over to dismount. My leg was pinned between his leopard-spotted belly and the tin flashing on the corner of the barn. Ouch! I could feel the slice. Charlie moved away in response to my shout. I bent over and pulled up the pantleg of my jeans. Sure enough, there was a big gash on my right leg and the blood was flowing.

Dad had me at the Sunderland Hospital's emergency room in a flash. He said I'd need stitches but he wouldn't do the procedure. I wanted him to fix my leg. He said another doctor would have to do the job. It was Harry Pullin, a young guy doing his doctor experience with my dad. I wasn't sure he was up to the task, especially as his hand shook when he stuck a big needle into the side of my calf to freeze it.

I was bawling but Dad was there. Harry seemed nervous stitching me up. I think it was because Dad had his serious face on and Harry knew he was there to oversee things.

I felt broken. I wondered if I would ever be the same. Dad said not to run on the playground for a few days. He reminded me of this a week later when he plucked the stiches out of my leg. He said there were eight stiches. It seemed to me that there were more than that.

I spent days on the playground watching my friends running around, wanting things to go back to the way they were, when I could run like a deer.

I was convinced I would never be as fast again.

. . .

Dad was once injured quite badly by one of the horses. He was riding around the riding ring on Rio when suddenly Rio's rear legs slid out from underneath him. The horse ended up on top of my dad's legs. Dad suffered two breaks in his left leg. Two pieces of hardware were screwed into his bones. And while I was worried about Dad, my 10-year-old brain couldn't help but worry more that our planned trip to Disneyland was a goner.

Dad insisted that we would go. In a full-length leg cast and with crutches, in the August heat of California, Dad hobbled around Disneyland to see that his kids got the experience he'd promised us. I vividly remember that the one ride he wanted to go on with us was The Pirates of the Caribbean. But after dad had manoeuvred himself into the ride's floating car, the only way he could sit was to stick his leg outside of the car. The attendant said it wasn't safe, so dad had to get out and wait while we went on the ride.

I can't say I always went to the same lengths for my daughter as my father did for his children, but I can say when push came to shove, I tried. Thanks, Dad.

. . .

Through the years many village kids got introduced to horses through my parents, some pursuing the interest their whole lives. And while many said they were grateful for the opportunity my parents afforded them, my parents were always grateful in return for the help they received down at the barn.

Once I got to be about 15, helping at the barn became something I tried to avoid. I was much more interested in hanging out with my friends, riding our trail bike, and thinking about girls.

When the right opportunity presented itself, Dad would always tell the story about the time he tried to get me down to the barn to ride.

"I'll bet you five bucks you can't go over a couple of cavallettis on Joker Zeke," he said, adding, "You've probably forgotten how to jump a horse since you haven't been down to the barn in so long."

I liked the idea of five bucks.

"Okay, I said, "I'll ride the trail bike down to the barn tonight if you can have Joker saddled up ready to go."

Dad said he and a few of the barn rats were waiting for me when I arrived. He said I strode up to him, took Joker's reins, threw them over Joker's head, and mounted. After a quick trot around the ring, I steered Joker towards the cavallettis. Up and over we went. I continued at a trot right up to Dad, dismounted, and handed him the reins.

"Where's my five bucks?"

XII

For all the times I may have disappointed my dad, he never gave up on me. And when I really needed his wisdom and support, it was there. Like the time I banged up his truck.

Jerry Peillo (Cal called him Jerry "Pees Low," which made everyone laugh and caused Jerry's face to go red) heard the news on *Breakfast with Browne*. I wasn't thrilled to hear that it had been broadcast on local radio. When I arrived at school the day after the accident, Jerry couldn't wait to catch me in our Chemistry 11 class.

"Moore, you idiot, what did you do? Exactly how many hours did it take for you to get in an accident after getting your driver's licence?"

The answer was four hours. I had been out for a drive in my dad's GMC truck in the late afternoon, out on the "dump" road. Going around a corner at the speed limit of 50 kilometres per hour (no, despite the rumour I was not going 80 kilometres an hour), I hit a patch of ice. With my inexperience, I cranked the steering wheel too much. The truck spun around, the front went into a bank, and the vehicle flipped onto its side. I was thrown to the passenger side of the truck. With my head against the passenger door window, I could see gravel moving past before the truck came to a stop. I stood on the window, grabbed the steering wheel to pull myself up, and managed to push the driver's door open to get out.

It seemed like just seconds went by before some guy in a car pulled over.

"Do you need any help?" he said, as his eyes wandered from me to the truck, which was on its side, with its rear end sticking out onto the road.

"No, I always park my truck like this," I said, espousing the bravado of an idiot 16-year-old.

Thankfully, he just laughed and offered to phone my mum and explain the situation as soon as he got into town.

It must have been about an hour later when a tow truck showed up with Mum in the passenger seat. Her tone changed from a caring, "Are you okay," to subtle nonverbal communication that I recognized as, "What did you do this time?" once she realized I was fine.

It was taking longer than anticipated for the tow truck driver to sort things out so Mum was getting worried about Lena being picked up in Clifton. The driver patched Mum through on the CB to his company's switchboard and from there we were connected to Calvin, who was at home, anxiously awaiting the good news of how his younger brother had screwed up.

The connection was super staticky.

Mum: "Calvin, Stu has been in an accident." Crackle . . . crackle . . .

Calvin: "Is the truck okay?" Crackle . . . crackle . . .

Mum: "Everything is going to be okay. Listen, I really need you to drive down to Clifton to pick Lena up." Crackle . . . crackle . . .

Calvin: "I don't wanna."

The tow truck driver couldn't help himself. He burst out laughing. He quieted when Mum gave him a look. Oh, I thought. Her superpowers work on other people, too.

Anyway, it was soon sorted out. Cal picked up Lena.

I could see my dad's new, white VW fastback in the driveway as the tow truck driver turned onto our street to drop us at home. Dad was sitting at the kitchen table when we walked in. He asked what happened. I offered a quick summation before I broke down.

"I'll never drive a car again, Dad, I swear," I said tearfully.

"YES, YOU WILL," he said in a strong tone. He reached into his pocket, pulled out the keys to his new car, and threw them across the room to me. "You get in my car right now. And you go for a drive. I don't want to see you back here for half an hour. Now get going."

XIII

The old elementary school that I attended until Grade 3 was an amazing structure, at least in Sunderland environs. Basically across the street from our home, on a high point of land, it demanded your attention with its two levels of classrooms and tall, pointed bell tower, from which a loud bell would ring to summon you from your playground play. But . . . it was a relic, having been constructed in 1898.

The steps that we lined up in front of to wait for our Grade 1 teacher, Mrs. Milson, were steep and treacherous. Once when exiting the school I tripped at the top and took a nasty tumble. I was lucky to avoid a broken bone.

My biggest medical problem to that juncture of my life, with the exception of my previously diagnosed "dirtification," was the wart on my right index finger. Why, I could stare at it all day, all the while trying to remember the last time I'd touched a frog. According to Cale, you got warts from frogs. Cursed wart. How could I possibly focus on my *Fun with Dick and Jane* reader?

> *"See me jump," said Dick.*
> *"Oh my! This is fun.*
> *Come and play.*
> *Come and do what I do.*

Look, look!
Who can jump?
Who can do what I do?
"I can jump," said Jane.
"I can jump," said Mother.
"I can jump," said Father.
"See me jump," said Sally.
"I can jump and play."
"No, Sally," said Dick.
"You can not play.
You are too little.

One day at recess, I ran home from school in tears. I was a little sick but mainly upset about the wart. Mum helped me take off my blue jacket, the one with the kind of spongy material that has long disappeared from the kid jacket market. I surmise the material was highly flammable.

She sat me down next to her on the couch in the TV room. With her arm around me, I cried and cried out how sad I was. Pretty much the whole time, she rubbed a hand up and down the wart-inflicted finger. I believe I was hypnotized into believing that somehow it was nothing to be concerned about and that it would soon disappear.

My mother died recently at age 96. There are tears now at writing these words, as I know there will be in Port Orange, Florida, and in Brisbane, Australia, when my brother and sister read these words.

• • •

"Mum, why did you call me Stuart?"
"Well, when you spell your name backwards, what does it spell?"
I was an active little boy.

. . .

I can't recall whether it was in Grade 1 or Grade 2 when I caused quite a stir in my neighbourhood. It all started with my fascination with Jack Walston's huge collection of little green plastic army men. There were snipers, infantrymen, bazooka men, and an array of others; more than enough to create an amazing battle scene. Not that I'd seen them all at one time. Jack brought just a few to school each day with him. There would usually be a crowd of little boys around him at recess to see what he'd brought that day.

Jack had moved from Sunderland down to a home his dad built down in Alston. So, he rode the bus to school every day. I thought that must be neat. One day when he suggested I come to his house after school I couldn't say no. I followed right out of class and on to the bus. Sooo cool. I'd never been on a school bus before.

Jack's mom met us at the top of Garson Beach Road, where the bus dropped us. She seemed surprised to see me. It was like she wasn't expecting me. Nevertheless, within minutes we were in Jack's kitchen having a snack and soon got down to playing with Jack's army men collection. I was in heaven.

After an hour or so, Mrs. Walston asked me when my mum was picking me up. I told her I didn't know, because I DIDN'T KNOW. Mrs. Walston must have phoned my mum because she arrived soon after. Mum was not happy. In fact she was fuming mad. She'd had the neighbours and the staff at the school looking all over for me when I didn't return home from school that day. She was just about to phone the police when she received the call from Mrs. Walston.

. . .

While in Mrs. Couture's Grade 2 class there were a few weeks when the ceiling plaster routinely dropped on our class as we did our arithmetic or what have you. One day, Mr. Ferguson, the village dogcatcher, dropped his daughter Joan off in the hallway. At first I didn't notice the authentic man-sized safety helmet that adorned Joan's head, which was surprising because it looked ridiculous. I was transfixed with Mr. Ferguson's presence. I had seen him park his van near a village dog, open the rear doors to remove a wire noose attached to a pole, and lower the noose around the dog's neck, tightening it to the point the dog choked when he pulled the dog to the van. I hated him.

Joan wore the helmet proudly into the class, oblivious to the fact that it was just something else that some kids in the class would use to bully her about. It had taken me awhile to conclude that the commonly spread tale of her passing fleas on to others was just nonsense.

Mr. Ferguson had made his point. There was a hastily organized meeting at the end of the school day between teacher, principal, and parent. Regrettably I can't report the minutes, and I didn't notice anything different by the time I'd moved on to Grade 3.

Mrs. Tatum was firm. We knew that she didn't put up with much tomfoolery, which was rather unfortunate because I was quite good at tomfoolery, and I had hoped to teach others the dark art. Not only did she have high expectations for our behaviour within the classroom, she expected us to be presentable. Much to my discomfiture, she would routinely inspect our fingernails, banishing anyone with dirty fingernails to the washroom. Readmittance to the classroom required passing an inspection that indicated the dirt had been sufficiently expunged.

· · ·

It must have been around Grade 2 when Cal and I first went to a dentist. There was no dentist in Sunderland when we were boys. But that didn't get in the way of my dad making sure we got to experience needles and the dentist's drill. He'd arranged for us to see Dr. Lyndon in Clifton. I must admit, I was excited to go the first time. In fact, I couldn't wait! I'd heard Mum's stories about Aunt Lil and her teeth . . . or lack of them. Aunt Lil was my mum's Scottish aunt. She lived down island in Chemainus. She'd visit every once and awhile. She must have been a Scottish gypsy, since Mum said her family were tinkers back in Scotland. Mum said in Scotland they called gypsies, tinkers. They moved from place to place in horse-drawn caravans, pausing for a time in different villages to mend villager's pots and pans, and to sharpen knives. I'd keep a close eye on Aunt Lil whenever I was aware she was in the kitchen. I wanted to see her mend a pot or sharpen a knife.

Whenever Aunt Lil would visit, Mum would make everyone some tea with loose tea leaves. Mum would make a big deal that Aunt Lil read tea leaves. Like with a lot of "first times," I was excited. But at least in this case it wasn't long before I felt a little let down. She pointed out a clump of leaves in my cup, saying she could see I was going to hit a baseball really far. At least that's what I think she said. It was quite a challenge to understand her with that Scottish lilt of hers. The scattered tea leaves looked more to me like Spike with one of his girlfriends.

I'd stare into her mouth when she talked, trying to determine exactly how many teeth she had left. Mum said Aunt Lil had never ever been to a dentist, and that she routinely pulled a tooth out with pliers when it was too far gone. I didn't want to be faced with that, so I couldn't wait for my first dentist appointment.

Like Dr. Ricks, I had a pretty good impression of Dr. Lyndon when I first met him. But when I found out he also had needles, our relationship changed. That old vibrating drill didn't help matters either. In the beginning my dad was tapped to take us to the dentist. I think Mum knew how things were going to evolve. She'd seen Number Two Son in action before. Anyway, the first few times my dad was called in from the waiting room in attempt to calm me down. Eventually Dr. Lyndon seemed to have the "do what you gotta do," from my dad, so a couple of extra dental assistants appeared and held me down.

I've certainly felt a lot of anxiety over the years prior to and during visits to a number of different dentists. I think my present dentist, Dr. Lusby, puts me into some kind of hypnotic trance. He denies it, but there must be something going on since I always feel comfortable during office visits.

I know, I know. Dr. Lusby will probably want to use my name in an advertisement once I'm a best-selling author. I have no idea what to charge.

Cal had fantastic teeth. Straight. White. He hardly ever got a cavity. On the other hand, one of my front teeth needed straightening since it interfered with my bite; at least that's what Dr. Lyndon said. The thought did cross my mind that he just wanted to torture me with some other procedure.

I ended up with a silver tooth . . . a silver cap over one of my front teeth. I soon found out that the initial boost to my self-esteem would be short-lived. I had started off feeling special because I had a reflective tooth. But after a few days on the playground, I felt as if I was an ugly duckling. Sometimes just having a difference pointed out was all it took.

Do you remember a time during your childhood when you looked into the mirror and didn't really like what you saw? I do. I was upset about my ears. They stuck out. In my mind I'd magnified the "flaw," to the point that I could see the ears of Dumbo the Flying Elephant in my reflection. Mum said they weren't that bad. I asked Dad how he got ears that stayed flatter against the sides of his head.

He said, "I don't know. I think over time when you sleep on them at night they just flatten out."

For the next several nights, I'd lie down in my bed at night and tuck one ear against the side of my head, and then the next night I'd do the other.

. . .

My memories
They come to me
I go back to that time
Back to that place

In the winter, at school recess and after eating lunch, my friends and I would head over to a corner of the playground near the high school's Industrial Education building. There was a special spot there where snow and ice would freeze and unfreeze, then curl around, creating the most fantastic ice slide. I swear the ice was crystal clear; even though it was about 10 centimetres thick you could see the dirt and grass below it. Only the brave and foolish would try to slide down it standing up. Many tried, few made it to the bottom without falling and suffering bruises or fractures. I don't know if some do-gooder squealed to the office, or if the office secretary became concerned after a series of wounded soldiers reported in for repairs, but at any rate one day the slide disappeared. We suspected some darn do-gooder school district employee had dosed it with salt.

Alas, all good things must come to an end. After many years of service the old school was torn down and the students of Sunderland would never ever hear the clang of a real school bell again. It would be buzzers thereafter. Annoying buzzers.

Grade 4 came along in the building that had been the old high school, the high school–aged kids having been moved up to the newly constructed junior high.

Grade 4 was memorable for two reasons. First, it was the only time I'd ever seen anyone fall right on his own face . . . without being pushed or anything. Cale and I were in a line of about six kids standing at the front of our seated classmates, taking turns reading aloud from our *Happy Highways* reader. Suddenly, Cale fainted. He fell straight forward, landing with a loud smack. We rushed to help him up. Once on his feet, he was kind of stunned and his lips were bleeding pretty good. That lucky dog got to go home for the whole day. My classmates and I had no reason to suspect he was faking it. Our go-to explanation whenever anyone went home sick was that they were faking it to avoid something.

The second memorable event was my first strapping, delivered with enthusiasm by our vice-principal Mr. Robson, aka "Stubby." I mean . . . come on people. All I had done was assemble a number of words in the rhyming form of a poem. Admittedly, um, I used inappropriate slang words for various private parts. Richard Jones took it upon himself to snatch my rough draft and take it to Miss Brown. That snitch! It didn't matter that he'd recently gave me a great deal, selling me a pair of soccer boots for two bucks. I was choked at him. He'd broken our code. I can only assume he was behind in points in the teacher's eyes and he wanted to improve his score. Miss Brown must have been sufficiently shocked upon reading my prose, or perhaps it was my illustrations that offended her sensibilities. She sought consultation with the administration, which sealed the deal. I would get the strap. So ended my career as a poet. I thought.

As it turned out, I wrote another poem a year or so later. My inspiration was the shocking sneak attack by wrestler Gene Kiniski on my favourite wrestler, Mark Lunam (the master of the "sleeper" hold). The whole disgusting affair played out before my eyes one Saturday afternoon on KVOS TV's All Star Wrestling. I was so upset I . . . I . . . wrote a poem about it. Quite a good one, I thought. And . . . I was determined to give it to Mark Lunam in person when he and a group of All Star Wrestlers visited Clifton's Recreation Association hall the following week. Mark didn't show! I was so disappointed. After all the matches were over I approached the lone man left in the ring . . . the referee.

"Where was Mark Lunam tonight?"

"Oh, hi, son. He wasn't feeling well so he didn't make the trip."

"I have something for him; could you get it to him?"

"What is it?"

I hadn't anticipated how embarrassed I would feel to tell him that I'd been upset about what happened to Mark a week earlier and so I'd written him a poem. And I definitely couldn't have anticipated the look the guy gave me after I handed it to him and said, "Pleeaassse, give it to him."

Sooo . . . the aforementioned strap, for those of you who have never had the pleasure, was a long, hard piece of rubber. I'd say about 60 centimetres long by five centimetres wide and one centimetre thick, although it is hard to make an accurate dimensional estimate when it is flying towards your outstretched hand, having been swung by a full-grown man who is not particularly happy with you, and granted the authority in those days to inflict physical punishment.

I think I got two on each hand, which was sufficient to start me balling my eyes out. But that was just the warm-up act. When I got home and my father had returned from work he reiterated that "If you get in trouble at school you get it twice as bad at home." It wasn't really as bad as it sounds and my father certainly wasn't an abusive sort. However, let's just say my bare backside could commiserate with the experience my hands had endured earlier in the day.

Dad expected his kids to be respectful and behave at school. He'd done a stint as a teacher in a prairie schoolhouse near Minnedosa,

Manitoba. Finishing school early, he'd done a year of Normal School training (that's what teacher training was called back then), and was teaching at age 17! We'd heard the stories of how it was a challenge teaching a multi-grade classroom, particularly when he had some older farm boys that were much bigger than he.

I digress here to add that it was while Dad was a teacher he first met Mum. It was a thing in those days for students to invite their teacher over for dinner. One year, Auntie Jean was a student of Dad's. According to Dad, he was surprised that when he arrived at the farmhouse for dinner the cook was a real good looker . . . Mum. Many years later I asked Dad what it was about Mum that really caught him. He replied, "Well, when she danced, she put everything into it. . . if you know what I mean!"

Anyway, my parents weren't serious proponents of corporal punishment. I can count on the fingers of my right hand the number of times that I got a licking, which is probably five times more than my siblings ever got. But Mum and Dad had their ways.

My dad could get my brother and I to jump with a well-delivered raised voice. And for the record, if delivered, it was for good reason. If the voice didn't work he might threaten the "shoe." The shoe hardly ever came off, and I can assuredly claim first place in having it come off many more times than my siblings. Just the threat of it usually got the desired result. My dad had big feet. A quick swat with a size 12 shoe on your backside was well remembered.

My mother preferred the "wooden spoon." I can still conjure the sounds of the kitchen utensil drawer being yanked open and my mother's hand noisily moving items around to find and grasp the wooden spoon. I'm sure she made an extra effort to rattle things around so that we knew she meant business. Even if at that juncture someone yelled, "I did it, Mum. I did what you asked," she would still appear before us brandishing the king of punishing utensils. Most of the time she'd just wave it around with a stern look on her face. It was rarely used, but the entire performance was very effective.

Ha! Years later after returning home from our respective universities on a spring break, Calvin and I got into an argument that got out of hand. I can't recall for certain but it might have had to do with the time I phoned a girlfriend's place and Calvin answered the phone! I was not happy about that.

Cal got me into a headlock, which was pretty much his only move. It was like a grip of death because at the time he weighed more than 90 kilograms, and he probably didn't know it . . . but he was strong. Whenever we returned from university we'd go to work at a pulp and paper mill north of Clifton. Because of his size, Cal was assigned to work in the infamous groundwood plant. All shift long, he'd use a short pike pole to pull large pieces of stumps off a conveyer belt. They created a monster.

Despite the fact Cal had me more or less immobilized, I fought on, tripping him, so that we both ended up on the carpeted floor. We rolled around, me in the impossible position of having big brother with a determined grip on my head. I was pushed halfway under the coffee table and starting to think it was a goner, when Cal and I heard the kitchen drawer open. Suddenly the grip on one of my more prized possessions (my head) was released. A 90-kilogram-plus man ran down the hallway to escape the potential consequence of the wooden spoon, something imprinted in his brain years before.

. . .

Mentioning our employment at the mill, I can't help but recall how it came about in the first place. I had a friend who had scored a job at the mill. These jobs were prized because they were the highest-paying jobs available for young fellas. He told me it was hard to be given serious consideration unless you spoke with the personnel manager, one Mr. Short . . . Mr. Larry Short. And to make things more challenging, it was difficult to get past the watchman at the main gate.

I was determined. Once I arrived at the mill I parked and walked right past the front watchman, "like I owned the place." To show my confidence, I didn't even glance at him but walked straight ahead with a serious look on my face, like I had to get to an important meeting. I might have looked a bit ridiculous. I don't know how frequently skinny 17-year-olds were invited to important meetings by the mill's administration.

Once I got into the mill proper, I could see a sign that read "Personnel Office." I strode up to it, paused to gather myself before entering, and then walked in. There was a cranky-looking receptionist there. She looked even crankier when she looked up from her work.

"Can I help you, young man?" she inquired, politely enough.

"I'm here to see Mr. Small," I said belying my nervousness.

"I'm sorry, young man, there isn't any Mr. Small here."

"Look," I said, "I know what you're doing. I know a lot of guys come in here to see Mr. Small. But I really need to see him."

"Like I said, there's no Mr. Small here."

There was a lot on the line for me. I needed to make some dollars for university. And so I raised my voice and pushed matters. "I'm not leaving here until I see Mr. Small . . . MR. LARRY SMALL!"

"Ohhh, you mean Mr. Short," she said.

We both noticed the rather diminutive man entering the room from a hallway.

"Why . . . here he is," she said.

Instantaneously, I realized I'd made a complete ass out of myself.

"Come on in," he said.

Well, it turned out okay. Mr. Short complimented me on my determination, and to a lesser extent on the entertainment I'd provided. I was hired and assigned to Number Three Pulp Machine.

When I returned home, Cal was jealous that I'd scored such a great job. He wanted one too.

"What do I have to do to get a job there? I heard it's tough," asked Cal.

"It's not that hard," I reassured him. "Just walk through the main gate . . . confidently. Head to the personnel office. AND, this is the important part. Ask to see Mr. Small. Don't take no for an answer."

We were both lucky to get those jobs at the mill. We returned every summer while we attended university and sometimes put in a few shifts when we were home for the holidays during the year. I was mostly assigned to be utility man on Number Three, despite the fact that I shut down the mill's entire pulp production for a few hours after I plugged up the pulp recycler, on account of not keeping an eye on it, adding water when I should have to soften the sheet of pulp so it could be chewed up by giant blades. There were quite a few mill "bigwigs" running around the Number Three building when it all came down. I was told the shutdown of production cost the company a lot of money.

For Cal's part, he was pretty much resigned to the fact that every time he returned to work at the mill he'd get the brutal assignment of Groundwood. He'd go right to bed after his first few shifts every summer until he got in fighting shape.

Ha, ha, ha! Poor Cal. Often we'd have a party lined up on a Friday night and the phone would ring sometime after dinner. I think I saw Cal wince on a few occasions upon hearing it. Mum would answer the phone and the conversation was pretty much the same every time.

"Hello, Moore residence. Yes, yes, he's here. Just a moment."

Cal would take the phone.

"Hello, Cal speaking."

"Moore, we need you to cover for someone tonight. Groundwood . . . 12 to eight." Meaning Cal would have to leave the party very early, change, and be prepared to work all night from midnight until eight in the morning.

XIV

Now Mrs. Mackle was a gem for Grade 5. If you could see past the outer . . . can I say "gruffness" without offending any of her previous students? She'd seen it all in her years in the trenches. She certainly had my number. See actual first-term report card comment:

"Stuart is a bright boy when he pays attention, but he sure likes to monkey around if you let him."

Luckily, there was no known significant punishment in the Moore household for being likened to a primate in a report card comment. Although I'm confident an eyebrow was raised.

Mrs. Mackle taught me a great deal about what I could accomplish if I was focused. She provided the framework. I wasn't yet able to self-manage. There is no doubt that her efforts helped me to become a better student.

I sat in the row of desks beside a series of windows, which would all be pushed up and opened in the late spring. The class would have a frequent visitor . . . a crow. It started with fleeting visits to a window ledge, which gradually increased in duration. It seemed he was watching the goings on in the class. I decided that social studies seemed to be his favourite subject. Anyway, he upped the ante. At first we were unaware that he was actually entering the class to hop along the top shelf that ran along just under the windows, and taking pencils and erasers that had been left on the shelf. We believed we had a thief from outside our classroom of kids, but Mrs. Mackle let us know she believed it was one of us. I had every confidence that she would soon nail the culprit.

Well, we caught the crow in action one day while we were working quietly in our notebooks. Someone let out a shout . . . all eyes were on the crow hopping back to the window ledge and flying off, clutching one of those pink erasers that smelled funny and left little pieces of brown rubber when you used them. Those of us with prime window seats saw him fly towards a row of mature maple trees. There were four or five of these large-circumference trees. They'd obviously been pruned for years on end because at about two-and-one-half-metres tall the old growth stopped, and from there several small branches grew up. Evidently it was a perfect cache for our un-litigated suspect.

After school one day, before Mrs. Mackle could get around to it, I decided to apply my innate primate skills and climb the closest tree. I succeeded! Low and behold, there was a nest about a 45-centimetres wide containing an impressive collection of pencils and erasers. Apparently, our crow had not restricted his activities to just one classroom.

Not long after, our crow disappeared, seemingly overnight, as our ice slide had. Hmm. Once again we suspected the authorities.

. . .

Mrs. Mackle taught me an important lesson in spelling class that went far beyond spelling words correctly. We had just finished our spelling test, completed on that coarse brownish foolscap that Mrs. Mackle had torn lengthwise to save paper. As we usually did, our papers were passed to the person in front of us for marking (except the student at the front of the row . . . he or she had to walk their paper to the student sitting at the rear). We'd each take out our red pencil for marking, but inevitably someone had misplaced theirs, which would delay the proceedings until Mrs. Mackle found one for loan in her wooden desk (the desk you would not approach unless directed to).

"Children, this is why we have to keep our materials organized."

The process would start.

"Number one . . . "disappointed." I was disappointed to see rain clouds this morning."

Hands would shoot into the air. Mrs. Mackle would select a student to spell the word out loud. "Stuart!"

"Disappointed," I said aloud: d-i-s-a-p-p-o-i-n-t-e-d."

Each word would receive a check mark or a cross, depending on whether it had been spelled correctly or not. At the end, we'd tally the student's score and record it at the top of the page. On this particular day, I had marked the paper of a student who was new to our class. He scored only three words correct out of 15. I was shocked and blurted the score out. Mrs. Mackle was by my side in seconds. She didn't say a thing, nor did she need to. I just knew I'd done something wrong. I'd humiliated the new student.

I took the lesson with me; when I became a teacher, I always attempted to spare my students from any attention that could humiliate them in front of their peers.

. . .

With spring came preparations for the Maypole Dance on Empire Day, the celebration of the Queen's birthday. Mrs. Mackle would line us up outside of the school and with her at the lead we'd set off. Down towards the Sunderland Recreational Institute hall we would follow. Making a sharp left on to the main street, on we would go for the seven or eight blocks until reaching the big park at the end of town. There, several maypoles had been erected for us to practice with.

I took a little detour one day. I don't know what possessed me but when we reached Tarbell's Hardware Store, I just couldn't resist the open door. I left the line and entered the store. The lady working behind the till inquired if I might need some assistance. As I was formulating a brilliant answer, my left hand was suddenly grabbed, and I was spun around rather sharply, by ye old battle axe. Mrs. Mackle was not pleased. That was not a good thing. I think it was the last time I ever left a line. I suppose most students learned to stay in line long before they were 10 years old.

When we reached the park, we would be instructed to rearrange our line so that males and females alternated, and then we were led around the circumference of a maypole. Now you may have seen a proper well-executed maypole dance: nicely dressed smiling children, twisting in and out as they passed one another, making a beautiful plait at the top of the pole as a result of weaving their respective ribbons, held high in hand . . . but the first few days of practice were anything but that. And, I will leave it at that! One could see the veins popping out of Mrs. Mackle's forehead.

But we would be ready when Empire Day came and perform our dance to the well-worn recording played over the speakers with accompanying distortion and static. At the end of the dance, each child would have a dime pressed into the palm of his or her hand. How rich must the village be, I wondered, if they were giving money like this away to every child taking part in a maypole dance.

Our dance would have been just one of the activities of the Empire Day celebration. Lots of different activities took place down at the park. I always looked forward to the track events like high jump, broad jump, and the foot races. A guy could win a dime or two.

And I always looked forward to the hamburgers with lots of onions, and pop and candy floss! Many volunteers composed of parents, teachers, and other village folk worked frantically to serve the patrons who lined up in front of their booths.

Of course things had kicked off earlier with a parade, complete with all kinds of floats, Scottish marching bands, groups carrying banners, and children dressed up on their decorated bicycles. Oh, and there were firetrucks, whose sirens would make you jump and babies cry.

I have a photograph from one parade somewhere stored in a cardboard box in my basement. I am standing on a float (in this case, essentially the back of a flatbed truck decorated to look like a Hawaiian scene) with Stuckle Stevenson. I guess I got off easy. I am shirtless and wearing a pair of flowery shorts. I stand in a warrior like pose, clutching a spear. Poor Stuckle is dressed as a hulu girl, complete with grass skirt, lei, wig, and bikini top.

. . .

I used to bend the tops of trees
They'd lay me gently to the ground.

I drove by the old family home in Sunderland just the other day. Pulling the car over, I spontaneously recalled some stories associated with the house to tell my wife about. I'm not entirely sure, but I think she was bored. Sometimes she is a good actress; maybe it's a useful trait for surviving a marriage with me.

The tree . . . it used to be a shrub . . . on the street side of the front deck was hopelessly overgrown. It must have been 12 metres tall. I used to jump from the deck, grab the top of the shrub, and bend it to the ground. Am I more amazed at its present height, or at the very fact that it survived my abuse?

As we drove down the hill, I see that it's still there—that magnificent old deciduous tree on the other side of the house. I can't think what kind of tree it might be. Maybe something exotic, imported from England, and planted by the Englishman that first owned the house. My friends and I used to climb that tree regularly, reaching heights that terrified my mother. My father would use the opportunity to accuse my mother's lineage of recent descent from Order Primata, seeing that I seemed to enjoy spending my life in the tree. Completely not true! Yes, I did spend extraordinary periods of time in the tree, hanging by my tail, but I would come down every once and awhile, hungry, and venture to the kitchen for sustenance . . . a banana.

. . .

Eating a snack or a lunch got in the way of our playground fun at school. I don't think we would have eaten if there wasn't a rule that we had to wait for a period of time before getting dismissed. On the playground we played, "Hoop," a variation of, "Tag" (You're it!), where all those tagged stayed in the game until we got the very last speedster. All over the playground we would go—down by the sturdily built merry-go-round, where many a noggin was cracked or tooth dislodged—over by the Industrial Education building, and anywhere in between on the mostly pebbled school grounds. It was a huge playground and kids would be spread out all over it.

If you weren't careful, you could run between Pat Clancy and Timmy Randle, while they were trying to perfect their football spirals as they tossed the pigskin back and forth between one another. Pat could get pretty mad. I guess he had an Irish temper. *Such a dumb ball,* I thought. It wasn't even round. You could hurt your foot on it if you kicked it in the wrong spot and if you screwed up your catch, which was easy to do, it might deflect into your face; those ends of the ball sure could hurt. But that didn't stop me from being interested in football. Our team was the BC Lions and when Jack Walston showed up with his collection of colourful plastic Nalley's football coins—each picturing a different player like Joe Kapp or Willy Fleming—we crowded around. (Note to self: in the next life when Jack offers to sell you his coins for two cents per coin, take him up on it. I just checked eBay and there's a lot on there for $500).

Some days, we played softball in front of the decrepit metal and mesh backstop, over near the auditorium. It seemed the bats were huge and heavy, challenging to swing around in time to make contact with a pitch. I recall the day it was Turnip's turn to bat. I don't know if he'd already taken practise swings in the on-deck circle (there wasn't one formally demarked; we just knew where it was), but for some reason when he got into the batter's box he took a mighty backswing before a pitch was thrown. Unfortunately, Foo, who was bat catching at the time, was hit in the face. It's hard to erase the sound of the bat meeting one of his front teeth and knocking it plumb out of his mouth.

Over in one corner of the playground on a large, deteriorating cement pad was where we'd play Foursquare. Many games would be going on at once. Four players in, trying to get one another out. Several kids waiting for their turn to get in on the action. I'm sure our coordination and balance was challenged to develop because many of the foursquare courts had cracks, seams, or uplifted corners, which could cause a ball to suddenly bounce in a funny direction, making it hard to get your hands on it. Oh, and when it rained there would be puddles that you had to jump over as you played. We didn't mind the extra challenge but it sure was a pain if you had to return to class with a soaking wet sneaker.

· · ·

All the physical activity that a boy could engage in on the playground seemed a good thing. I recall an experience I had many years later when I worked in a local school. I was the only male staff member and only present in the school one day per week. The principal asked if I could look after a boy who had been suspended for the playground play part of lunch. I understood the kid before I met him. He had challenges with over-activity and impulse control. One on one, I found him to be a very likeable kid. We sat in my office for a few minutes and when the buzzer rang for the other students to come in off the playground, I suggested we go down to the gym.

"Go down to the gym?" he asked, surprised.

Once there, I grabbed a soccer ball from the equipment room and we went outside. We kicked the ball back and forth a bit. I started to lead him so he had to run to intercept the ball. He then started to lead me the same way. One of his kicks was hard and considerably off course. I had to break into a run to get to it.

"I've never seen a teacher run at this school before," he said.

How sad, I thought.

· · ·

At one juncture during my Grade 5 year, a new dynamic appeared, which I wasn't really ready for. Afterall, I was still into play with my male friends. At times relating to them cooperatively and at times trying to get one over on them before they got one over on me.

Girls were too ornamental. I can see Audra Stottard with her preened hair, white blouse, pink button-up sweater, pleated skirt, and those ridiculous black shoes with one skinny strap holding them closed. An absolutely unrelatable uniform to my eyes. Totally impractical for everyday playground use or for wrestling after school.

Eventually, the Grade 5 class caught hold of the dynamic that was going around the grade 6 and 7 classrooms like the Hong Kong flu. Everyone had to be, "going with," a member of the opposite sex. I didn't really know the details of what "going with," entailed but I was starting to feel pressure to conform.

I think it was Deanne Milton, a classmate of mine, who first broached the subject with me, suggesting her younger sister as a potential partner. I was confident I had discouraged her sufficiently, but one day there was a knock on the door of my house. My mother answered it. There was nine-year-old Cassandra Milton. I was called to attend the door from the TV room where my siblings and I were engrossed in another episode of *Jonny Quest*.

Mum left Cassandra and me alone to chat on the veranda. Soon, we were strolling down the cement walk beside my house (yup, she literally led me down the garden path) when Cassandra determined it was time to get down to business. Within minutes. she had me sold on the notion that it could be in our mutual best interest to be "going out."

I think the deal was just about closed . . . I didn't know how one finalized the arrangement, but I was pretty sure it didn't involve spitting in one's hand and shaking your promised one's, when my mother suddenly appeared. How did she always do that?

She asked what we were talking about. With a measure of pride, I informed her that Cassandra and I were now going out together. With clear and firm language, she let Cassandra and I know that our arrangement was null and void.

"Stuart isn't allowed to have a girlfriend until he is 18 years old," she said matter-of-factly.

Cassandra went on her merry way and I admit that this was a time I felt it was rather fortuitous that Mum had appeared.

XV

It seemed that hoodlums and lollygaggers doomed me to an anxious year in Stubby Robson's Grade 6 classroom. It was a time when children could be failed not once, but twice. I suspected three times since there were some large, intimidating characters in the class. And I recall Mr. McGinity's Grade 7 boys being lumped together with our boys for a subject or two.

Stubby taught us music, although I do not recall ever seeing a musical instrument.

> *I look up*
> *To the shining stars*
> *It's another lonely night*
> *On the planet Mars*
> *And I wonder, does she know I'm still in love with her?*

In class after class, Stubby would play a song on the phonograph and prod us to sing while he sat behind his desk, staring at us with exophthalmos eyes. How many times did we sing along to "Four Strong Winds?" Misbehaviour would be dealt with by the "pointer." Instructed to lean over a desk, Stubby would then administer the pointer stick across a delinquent's buttocks two or three times.

Compliance would almost certainly follow. I definitely sharpened up just watching another student get whacked.

· · ·

There are pretty ones
That can catch your eyes
Words sometimes spoke
Make you feel good inside.

Grade 6 brought the stirring of a young man's passion.

Diary entry, October 11, 1968: "I like Lorena best. Then Laura, then Audra, then Lynne." Apparently, Lorena was awarded number one status because at the bottom of the diary page, under the title of "Special Events," I wrote: "Sonora (Lorena) and them said hi to me today."

Things progressed, for a week later, October 18, 1968, I wrote, "I love Lorena, Laura, Audra. XXOXOXXOOOXXOO, and Lynne. I just love girls."

By November 16, 1968, I had declared: "My hobbies are swimming, skating, girl-watching, volleyball, soccer, football, and hockey. I am a playboy!"

Note to self: In your next life, be sure to hide diary in a better place so your six-year-old sister does not take it to school and show comments to identified love interests. Staring googly-eyed at girls is permissible, but love declarations in a diary once made public are not well received.

Thank you, Little Sister, for the important learning experience.

· · ·

As I have referred to previously, my friends and I often suffered under the leadership of some of the older village boys. Ah . . . but credit must be given where credit is due.

One day for library class, we were surprised to find that Stubby had been replaced by a voluptuous young female teacher, Miss Sterling. Hallelujah! There was a God. I had begun to doubt, for despite my extra prayers, Raquel Welch, in leather bikini as featured in the movie, *One Million Years B.C.,* had failed to appear in my bed on any night over the previous several weeks.

Miss Sterling, was, well . . . certainly sterling.

Early into our first class with her, one of the senior leaders of the "Sweathogs" (I can't remember who it was . . . my attention was on Miss Sterling) hatched a plan, and thankfully we were all prepped for implementation.

A book was located on the lowest possible shelf. Having memorized the title . . . quite a feat for a Sweathog . . . he approached Miss Sterling, seeking assistance in locating said book.

No sooner had Miss Sterling kneeled down and reached forward for the book when suddenly 12 or 13 front-row voyeurs, ignoring her personal space, all leaned forward for the best view, while several others in the back had to rely on their imaginations.

I was in the front group. I don't think I ever enjoyed a day of school as much. And it would be accurate to say that for a while my prayers were for a nighttime visit from Miss Sterling. Raquel Welch was temporarily demoted to second fiddle.

• • •

My memory suggests that the rest of Grade 6 was rather uneventful. I lament that Stubby upheld an exemplary attendance record and therefore I never saw Miss Sterling again. Well, at least not in real life.

Oh, there was the time the boys from Calvin's Grade 7 class joined ours. I don't know the reason why. Perhaps Mr. McGinity had been called away to a principal's meeting and Stubby got his boys while another teacher got his girls.

I have it now. I think we were lumped together to show our science projects.

Regardless, poor Cal. And poor Willy Solerton.

We grade sixers were in our seats. Calvin and Willy were at the front, I believe explaining their science project to the class. Suddenly, Calvin let fly a legendary upchuck of tentacle-like vomit that, while sticking to Willy's face in various locations, remained attached to my brother's mouth. Spiderman could do no better.

Willy let out a cry. Calvin's eyes were filled with stunned disbelief. Soon, gasps erupted from all witnesses, and shortly thereafter, as was typical, a couple of other kids vomited, but with much less creativity than my older brother.

Willy and Calvin were soon wiped down with paper towel and Cal was sent home, obviously legitimately sick. I couldn't wait to get home that day to tell Cal how awesome his performance had been, although upon informing him he seemed reluctant to accept my adulation.

In the years to follow, it became my go-to story whenever guys got together to tell gross stories, and I think it's fair to say I was the unofficial winner many a time. Thank you, brother, but I still want to know . . . how did you do that?

. . .

XVI

O thou with dewy locks, who lookest down
Thro' the clear windows of the morning, turn
Thine angel eyes upon our western isle,
Which in full choir hails they approach, O Spring!

—from To Spring by William Blake

Spring meant marbles. Regular glass ones containing a variety of colour swirls, similarly sized steelies, or the big bullfudgers. Breaks at school brought a flurry of playground activity. Set three in a row, mark a line a little over a metre away, and customers would arrive. Hit one of the marbles in the row and be rewarded with all three. Things went pretty much that way, day after day, until one day an innovation appeared. Bobby Walston, Jack's cousin, dug a wee trench and lined up a row of about 10 marbles. We flocked to this opportunity, even though his throwing line was two-and-one-half metres away! The temptation for a big score was too great. Game on. Marbles filled the air. His profits soared until, eventually, a happy participant scored a hit and collected the 10 marbles. It took us awhile to notice that Bobby collected at least 70 marbles during each marble storm. A lesson in entrepreneurial mastery.

When not engaged in marbles, springtime wrestling matches sprung up. Not so much during schooltime, since it was frowned upon. I, for one, had no intention of revisiting a strapping from Stubby.

I must have been on my way home from school since my match with Greig Montrose broke out just at the corner of our property, beside Bellemont Street, the one that led up to the New Houses. We were doing well, perhaps not worthy of inclusion on Ron Morrier's weekly *All-Star Wrestling* TV show, until a hand or a foot slipped, a temper was lost, and things escalated.

Seconds before further escalation brought us into donnybrook territory, we were interrupted by a loud horn. There at the corner of Bellemont and First Street was Tommy the Electrician in his van, the one with the slide-open front doors. His teeth broke their grip on his pipe and he laughed loudly. Reaching into his pocket, he withdrew his hand and threw a backhand into the air towards us. As his fingers opened a shower of coins were set free. The fight was over. There were plenty of silver coins for each of us. Enough for many trips to Mr. Beck's candy store.

. . .

Like most boys, I was conditioned by the television programs of the day to admire those in uniform, and so I was thrilled to be selected a captain on a newly created Crosswalk Patrol. Our uniform consisted of a bright yellow hard hat, safety vest, and handheld paddle with STOP emblazoned on it. On my weekly day of duty, my sergeant and I would proudly "march" down to the crosswalk that separated a far corner of the schoolyard from the block that was just steps away from Mr. Beck's candy store. With resolve, we'd perform our duty of protecting would-be candy purchasers, ensuring they safely got across the crosswalk and back to the schoolyard.

It would be two or three years later, at age 13, that I continued my, "military service," finally, receiving permission from my parents to join Army Cadets.

Cal had been with the Pigeons (Air Cadets) for a year and was really looking forward to the chance of steering an Argus, which was a marine reconnaissance aircraft. Eventually, he did. Foo had joined the Sea Lice (aka Sea Cadets) and was well into learning how to pilot a small sailboat. I wanted to join the Pongoes (aka Army Cadets), because I liked their uniform best.

I think my dad must have talked to Stuckle Stevenson's mom—she worked at the hospital—because it was arranged that Stuckle would pick me up on my first night. Stuckle arrived in uniform; I was impressed. Stuckle was a really good guy. Always jovial. We walked down to a spot in front of the post office and waited for our ride. Greig Montrose was there, as was his older brother, Billy. Billy had sergeant stripes on the arms of his tunic and he wore a real kilt. That was impressive! He seemed almost disinterested in his cigarette, but when a school bus pulled up he went to town on it before throwing it to the sidewalk, munching it with his big army boots, and then kicking it into the gutter. Six or seven of us loaded onto the bus. On to Clifton we went, picking up boys along the way, before we arrived at the military base.

After a short assembly of the uniformed cadets, the rookies were sent to the Stores Department to get uniforms. Now these were real uniforms. I mean, real! I think they were leftover supplies from the Second World War because they were the coarsest, itchiest trousers and tunic that you could imagine. My pants were too big at the waist; they just hung on me. My boots were too big as well. I didn't care. I was thrilled to have my uniform. I was, "in the army now!"

Of course, we had to keep our uniforms in tip top shape. Pants were to be pressed, hat badge shined with Brasso brass polish, and boots were to be shined to the point that, ideally, the reflection of the sun would blind. I had no idea how to shine army boots. I made the mistake of opening up that "can of worms," on the bus ride home. It seemed everyone had their own boot polishing technique, and most were very secretive about it.

In the weeks to follow, I wasn't having much luck with my boots. Luckily, Gumper, who was in Sea Cadets, shared his sure-fire technique:

Apply polish to boots with rag (Important! Don't use your socks)
Put boots in freezer section of refrigerator for two hours.

Remove boots and polish with soft rag, utilizing copious amounts of spit (spit was good for more than helping to shape a baseball mitt).

It worked! My boots started to get attention on parade night for their shine. Oh, and I got attention from my mother, when she discovered my boots in the freezer.

After about my third night at cadets I was starting to get the hang of, "Attention. Squad . . . turn right in columns of three. Turn right. Quick march. Squad, halt!" But apparently there was more to learn. At break time one of the older boys informed fellow rookie Neal Edwards and I that we had to go to see the commanding officer right away to ask for our "Mustardcation papers," or something like that. I didn't really hear it correctly and was unfamiliar with the word. Anyway, I ran along at double time behind Neal to the CO's office. Neal knocked on the door.

"Yes, cadet," said the CO.

Neal spoke dutifully, "Sir, we were told to see your immediately to get our Masturbation Papers."

Needless to say, I think the whole squad was waiting for us when we returned outside. They had a great laugh and razzed us for a couple of weeks. And I learned a new word.

. . .

I was having a difficult time getting a decent score at the indoor gun range on cadet night. The rifles were heavy and, to be honest, I'd had almost zero experience shooting.

True, there was the time I was waiting for Mum in our Ford Falcon, which was parked across the street from Maffetti's Grocery. I fired off a couple of shots from my pea gun at some old guy who was heading into the store. I got him. I know because when Mum returned from Maffetti's I was spoken to and my gun was confiscated.

Much to my embarrassment, the Gunnery Officer kept pointing out my incompetence. Stuckle, who was next to me, offered to help. He was a great shot, having had lots of experience while on several hunting trips in his young life already.

When the officer shouted, "Shoot . . . reload . . . shoot . . . reload . . . shoot," Stuckle squeezed off a couple of rounds at my target.

"Moore. Bullseye," the Gunnery Officer called out moments later. Stuckle smiled his big toothy grin. I smiled back.

XVII

Cal had a paper route in enemy territory: "Camp." More than once, he was "detained," by some kids that called "Camp" home. Camp was a long stretch of older cabins that had been owned by the mining company and rented out to employees. I suppose the kids that lived there weren't really bad kids. We both had friends that lived there, but they could be very territorial to be honest. An outsider on a shiny bike could be a target.

Cal had a bike stolen once. I went with him and my mum to report it to the little police station that used to be down by the firehall. The policeman took down some notes and told us he suspected it was probably stolen by someone from outside of town. We believed him because we knew nobody from town could ride that bike around without getting noticed.

One day Mum asked me to go along with Cal on his route. I didn't have a bike at that time. I'd hurriedly thrown my beloved CCM steed down on our driveway one day and rushed inside the house to catch *The Addams Family*, *The Munsters*, or some other intellectually stimulating program of the like. Mum backed up over it awhile later with the huge green Ford station wagon. It wouldn't be replaced right away. Sometimes a lesson needed awhile to sink in.

Anyhow, I went on foot, running when Cal was up to speed on his bike. I was fully prepared to back him up if necessary . . . maybe. Turned out that between the kids that I knew and the kids Cal knew we were granted safe passage.

While Cal had a paper route, I delivered the *TV Guide*, mostly to customers nearby and behind the hospital. Twenty-five cents would get it delivered to your door (I'd get to keep 10 cents or was it five?). Then you could fully prepare your TV viewing for the week and read an article or two on a TV star. It always peeved me that I'd find a show I wanted to watch and it would turn out that we didn't have that particular American TV station.

Not far after rounding the corner of the hospital I'd drop a Guide in Mrs. Casorzo's mailbox. She was a nice lady. She was Jack Walston's grandmother. Jack seemed to be there on occasion to say, "Hi."

Across the street I'd go to Uncle Arthur's and Auntie Phyll's. They weren't really my relatives. The Wamsleys were just good friends of my mum and dad's. Uncle Arthur was the postmaster in town and, let me tell you, he was one doozy of a badminton player. You'd never know it from looking at him, though. But he would dance around a badminton court on his toes and with a flick of his wrist propel a badminton bird seemingly wherever he wanted to. Auntie Phyll was a nurse. She had white, silky hair. Rumour had it that she kept my dad in line over at the hospital. Or maybe I extrapolated that idea from the fact that she always kept me in line. I assumed everyone else on the planet had to be kept in line from time to time. When it was my dad's turn, I just assumed it would be Auntie Phyll.

I'll get in big trouble for this one, especially when my book becomes an international bestseller! One time the doorbell rang at the Wamsleys'. Answering the door, Auntie Phyll found my sister Lena and her friend, Marie Dennie, standing there with a big bag of juicy, ripe cherries. Lena and Marie did their best pitch to sell them. They didn't have any luck. It turns out Auntie Phyll had been watching the girls, minutes earlier, pick the cherries from the tree in the Wamsleys' backyard.

Anyway, my *TV Guide* delivery career was soon over. You can't fake it. You have to believe in your product.

. . .

Funny how you could miss winter even though just a few short weeks earlier you were sick of it. Wet winter feet. Oh, how I hated those. But we missed the sledding. We missed the warped wooden toboggan that we couldn't steer, no matter how hard we tried; and the laughter that resulted from crashes where all three or four passengers would be thrown in every direction. Chaos was rewarding.

Cale and I were snooping around my basement looking for something to do. We spotted the toboggan leaning up in a corner, and simultaneously we were struck with the genius idea of inventing tobogganing in the spring. Clearly necessity—in this case, the want to escape boredom—truly is the mother of invention.

Well, we tried the front lawn. The small hill there had a significant grade, but we couldn't go far enough nor get enough speed up on the grass to reward with a decent ride.

I don't know who came up with the next idea. I'll say it was Cale, because there's been enough evidence of my work to lead you to a negative opinion of me.

The front stairs connected the large veranda on the front of the once grand house with the beginnings of the lawn and gardens, which were still pretty impressive in the 1960s. I'd seen pictures of the "well to do," members of 1920s village society mulling around on those wood steps and in the garden below participating in a Canadian version of a British tea party.

There was no debate that we were going to give it a try. The stairs were intimidatingly steep, so there would be no question of suitable momentum. We discussed who would sit at the front of the toboggan and who would be on the back. Obviously, Cale had determined that he didn't care to lose a tooth or two should we slam into one of the columns on yet another set of stairs that led down to a lower level of the garden. And so, after some resistance, punctuated by Cale referring to me as, "Chicken," I rose to the challenge. I would sit in front.

We positioned the toboggan at the top of the stairs. I sat down first in the front, tucking my legs into the curl of the toboggan. Then Cale sat down behind me. We started shimmying our derrieres to move the toboggan on the wooden deck, closer and closer to imminent death.

Finally, when a good part of the toboggan and, I suppose, me, was suspended in air, another shimmy did it. The front of the toboggan smacked down while the rear of the toboggan went up—suddenly and violently. Perhaps a millisecond before the toboggan started its trip down the stairs, Cale was thrown into the air over me and the front of the toboggan, landing in a crumpled heap about seven or eight steps down from me. He wasn't alone for long, though. The toboggan took off like a shot since the steps were so steep. I think Cale was just starting to moan from his unfortunate flight and landing when I, holding on for dear life, ran right over top of him.

They say we learn from our mistakes. Yes, sir.

. . .

My dad was the second youngest of 12 children and raised on a farm in Minnedosa, Manitoba. I hardly knew any of my relatives. Few came the great distance to visit on the Island, and I think we'd made one trip since my brother and I were old enough to remember. Flashback: sleeping in the back of a green 1960 Ford station wagon.

I used to ask Dad, who of his seven brothers and four sisters was the fastest runner? Who was the smartest? Who was the tallest? Etc. etc. until my father could take no more.

I knew only two things about my Uncle Joe when he appeared at our house one day. First off, he was a lot older than my dad, being third oldest of the brood and, secondly, on account of me paying attention to my dad's responses regarding family, I knew that Uncle Joe was kinda lazy.

Now my dad didn't exactly frame it that way. It went more like, "Hmmm, Uncle Joe. Well, Uncle Joe is the kind of guy that if there was something needing done on the farm, he'd sit and think about it for most of the day, and then come up with an easier way of doing it."

Of course, my dad did not explain that if one sits long enough, others will have done the work. I just surmised that Uncle Joe was . . . I don't know . . . some kind of inventor.

Unlike my dad, Uncle Joe had a long, slightly crooked nose. I seem to have that family gene. Of course, the conformation of my nose wasn't helped the time I was cutting alder firewood when a tree sprung up and disrespectfully moved my nose over a notch.

Uncle Joe most often had a rollie hanging out of his mouth, and he didn't seem partial to shaving every day or even every second day. Most of the time he wore one of those sloppy tweed hats, which in retrospect made him look like a stereotypical Irishman. He certainly had Irish blood.

Uncle Joe stayed for about a month in total. He was frequently late for dinner, having a measure of forgetfulness, I thought, and having made friends with some villagers down at the Maverick Hotel, which surprised me because Uncle Joe didn't talk a lot. I couldn't understand why he would talk less and less after 30 or 40 of my questions.

Round about a week into his stay, Dad put Uncle Joe to work building go-carts for my brother and I. I was surprised. He went right to it. And Uncle Joe had a carpenter's skill set.

The go-carts were uniquely designed, complete with new wheels and constructed with two-by-fours and plywood. Uncle Joe used some of the leftover red carpet and underlay from the new floor that had just installed in our living room.

I remember the day a group of men carried the big rolls of carpet into the living room and plunked them right in the middle of the room for the next day's installation. I didn't think long as I estimated the possibility of fitting into one end of the carpet roll. Sure enough, by lying on the floor, putting my arms over my head, I was able to wiggle into the roll. It took quite an athletic effort, but I managed to get about half way into the roll before I was exhausted and the circumference of the tunnel was somehow smaller. I was stuck. I began to feel claustrophobic. I called out for help. There must be some physics rule that explains how sound emitted in the centre of a carpet cylinder isn't carried very far, because no one heard my cries. It was terrifying.

After a while, my dad must have come looking for me because I hadn't responded when called for dinner. As he passed by the end of the roll, he heard my whimper.

Getting down on all fours, he looked into the roll and could see the top of his number two son's head. "What are you doing in there, Stuey?" he muttered.

He lifted one end of the carpet, which was a feat in itself, and moved the roll back and forth until I started to slide, ever so slowly, out of the roll. I was so glad to be free. I knew I would be in no hurry to crawl into a carpet roll again.

Anyway, Uncle Joe outdid himself. Our carts were carpeted, and the seats were so cushy because of the underlay!

On mine, I could sit on the cushy seat with my feet on the front two-by-four, steering by pushing one way or the other. Or, if I was in a daredevil mood, lie down on my stomach and steer with my hands. Either way was loads of fun, although there was the occasional tendency for the cart to flip. The pavement was hard!

So day in and day out we rode. Our go-carts were probably the picks of the litter of those that frequented Hospital Hill. There were some carts that would show up that had obviously been hastily slapped together. Well, at least their driver got a ride halfway down the hill.

But one day Cory Formier showed up with a real beauty. Cory, who was a bit of a little prick (he once informed me that my brand-new pair of snoot boots didn't suit me because I wasn't cool), had help from an older brother to make one mean machine. It was about twice as long as any other cart on the hill; long because it had to be to reduce the downward angle from the rear wheels, which were full-sized bicycle wheels. It had an actual cockpit with a steering wheel. That thing would go faster down the hill than seemed possible. It would have enough speed to make it through the dip and up the hill by the United Church. I suspect if he'd been interested he could have continued on through the stop sign by Beck's candy store and down another hill and around a corner by C. C. White's house, but of course then it would be one heck of a walk all the way back to Hospital Hill.

Hospital Hill delivered in the spring as well as in the winter.

XVIII

I don't know how I came by Timmy Randle's pellet gun on my lonesome, with half a pocketful of ammunition. It seems odd to me now that "Chunk" would have just outright lent it to me. Maybe it was one of those, "try before you buy promotions." I remember as clear as day standing alone in Moore's Forest, as excited as I could be to try the gun out. In front of me there was one of those common red berry trees, so common that of course I can't remember the name of it. It was about four or five metres high, replete with berries. Plump spring robins were flying all around it, pausing every so often to sit on a branch to feast.

"Puunnnkkk." I fired my first pellet. Nothing. I cracked the barrel open and inserted another pellet.

"Puunnnkkk." I got one. A robin fell to the ground.

I shot and reloaded, over and over.

There was no one around to say, "Stop it, you idiot," or other words of deterrence. I had been dreaming of shooting a real gun for a long time.

Eventually, I exhausted my pellet supply. I put the gun down and ran over to the tree. Horrified, there were robins scattered everywhere beneath it. I dragged a beat-up old car tire that I found close by over to the tree and started filling it with dead birds. There were 17 of them. Many with little blood spots where a pellet had penetrated their orangey-brown chests.

I was overwhelmed with shame. These years on, I can still feel it.

I didn't buy Chunk's gun, nor did I ever buy one. And I never shot an animal ever again.

. . .

Eventually I did buy something off the Randles, albeit several years later! It was the first car I ever purchased . . . a light grey 1960 Morris Minor, complete with seats that gave off an old leather smell. It had originally been owned by Uncle Arthur and Aunt Phyll. Mr. Randle had bought it for his sons to learn to drive with.

For $45 cash I scored the little four-banger that while great on gas, used engine oil like crazy. I joked with friends that I'd pull into a gas station and asked them to, "fill her up with oil and check the gas." One time I pulled over down by Camp with a flat tire and set about to change it. When I popped off the hubcap, I discovered that the wheel was being held on by just three of five lug nuts. I guess it was fortuitous that the car never went that fast.

After several months, I sold the car for $45 to Scott Ingles, a Clifton boy, who I knew through football. He ended up marrying a Camp girl, Wanda Baker. I'd wager that car was long gone by the time Scott first dated her. That car would have been a deal-breaker for sure.

. . .

My brother and I were lucky, although it didn't always feel that way, to have been exposed to various extracurricular activities. First up, when we were quite young, were Scottish dancing lessons. That didn't last long. After each class, my brother and I would both squawk all the way home from the Pioneers' Hall in Clifton, where the class was held. Additionally, I think both the dance teacher and my mother realized I didn't quite have the attention span at the time.

Next up was tap dancing at the Miners' Institute Building, not far down the road from home, located equidistant between Mr. Beck's and the unofficial entrance to Camp. It seemed more fun. "Ball, chain, ball, chain, shuffle, shuffle."

There's a photo kicking around somewhere of Calvin, Andy Stevens, and me in our sailor outfits. Neat little dark blue blazers with brass buttons and captain hats. We performed a little routine with three girls, who wore those little white dixie cup navy hats and what I assume were pretty little girl dresses. Still, we didn't stick with tap dancing very long.

Andy Stevens was in my brother's classroom. He was inseparable from his best friend, Waynie Muzik. Both of them lived up in the New Houses, just a hop, skip, and jump from one another via the alley that ran behind their homes. I was invited to come along once with my brother to a birthday party for Waynie. Lots of kids were there. Mrs. Muzik put on a real feed for us. It was then that I discovered that even a sublime hotdog could be improved upon. Mrs. Muzik served hotdogs smothered in fried onions.

And the cake! Mrs. Muzik baked Waynie's birthday cake herself. We were all cautioned to check our piece carefully before biting in. The cake was full of nickels and dimes! We thought that was something special.

Waynie had a Science Research Associates (SRA) kit in his bedroom, just like the one that we had in our classroom at school. It consisted of stories, each on a separate cardboard sheet, and arranged from easiest to hardest. After each story, your comprehension of what you had read would be tested. Also, you would be tested on your mastery of the vocabulary. It was designed for independent learning so you could mark your own when you'd finished. I used to like working with the kit at school because each sheet didn't take long to complete, and you got immediate feedback.

I'm sure that having his own kit helped Waynie in the long run . . . I know for a fact that he eventually forged a career as a writer and wrote and published at least two books.

Ha! Another birthday story. Calvin and I had been invited to Foo Cheung's birthday. Again, there were tons of boys there, which meant there was the potential for havoc, but Mrs. Cheung kept the proceedings well-organized. We played Pin the Tail on the Donkey, ate some great food, and watched Foo open his presents. At some point, one of the guys had gone to use the bathroom. He must have done some snooping around because he found a couple of skin mags that surely wouldn't have been left out for a group of 9- to 10-year-old boys to see. Mrs. Cheung must have thought that there was something amiss with the food she'd prepared because there was a constant stream of boys using the bathroom for the remainder of the party.

. . .

Mrs. McPherson lived in a large white house, located between the school and the Randles, about a five-minute sprint across the schoolyard from our house. She was our piano teacher. She was a very kind and patient teacher, charged with the task of teaching music to the Moore boys, who were most often distracted. My brother would have a lesson at 3:30 p.m. Tuesday, and I would have one at 4 p.m. The following week, we would flip time slots.

Why were we distracted at these particular times? Hmmm . . . let me rephrase that. Why was Calvin distracted at these particular times (you see, I was almost always distracted)? One of the greatest television shows that a 10- or 11-year-old boy could hope for, was on each Tuesday at 4 p.m. No, I'm not referring to *Hogan's Heroes*, *The Cisco Kid*, *The Lone Ranger*, or reruns of the late '50s *Superman* series . . . although they were of course, all-time greats that could draw 30 minutes of full attention from a 10-year-old. I'm talking about *Batman*!

"BAM . . . POW. . . WOW. . . " *Batman* with Adam West in the lead role and Burt Ward as Robin exploded on our colour TV. There was nothing like it! Even if Batman did look a little pudgy around the middle and appeared to have a hint of more breast tissue than one would expect for a superhero.

Our problem was the conflict between piano lessons and *Batman*! There seemed no greater challenge than to somehow resolve the unresolvable.

If you had the 3:30 p.m. lesson, you couldn't concentrate during the last part of your lesson since you knew EVERYTHING depended upon your ability to pack you music book up quickly and seek to establish a new sprint world record so that you only missed five minutes of the show. On the other hand, if you drew the 4 p.m. lesson, your fate was sealed. No *Batman* that week. How could you possibly focus on the difference between a quarter note and a half note when your thoughts were on *Batman*? Invariably one brother would inform the other on alternate weeks that the 4 p.m. lesson participant had missed the BEST EPISODE EVER. I would be furious at my mother when it was my turn to miss it. I recall mild-mannered Calvin being almost as angry when he had to tinkle the ivories and forgo the show.

XIX

Eventually Mrs. McPherson moved to Clifton, and two brothers, who I hereby nominate for the village's, "Hall of Fame, Fun and Quirky Character Category," moved into her old home with their foster parents and foster siblings.

Buzz and Gumper actually came to Sunderland pre-nicknamed. And they were appropriate nicknames too. Buzz, who was my age, was first off, not a neo-Nazi, although with his buzz cut he looked like one. That is to say his head was almost shaved, perhaps a solution to recurrent head lice infestations. Gumper, my brother's age, was, well, always doing gumper (entertaining, wacky, goofy) things. It is possible that they were both in the running for that particular nickname until the nickname Buzz became the obvious choice for the younger brother.

They became well-known within days of attending school. I always thought it was unfortunate that they were brothers and were together most of the time, because if Buzz screwed up, Gumper was guilty by close association, and vice versa.

Buzz had a little trick we'd never seen before. He would pull on the skin where his eyelashes attached to his eyelids and fold the skin up. You could see the inside of his eyelids . . . a pink strip, complete with blood vessels. It was enough to freak us out and we granted him our boyhood admiration for being so gross. The girls were horrified. Buzz would chase them, and we'd chase Buzz.

One day at lunchtime during his first week of attendance at our school, Gump put on a show for everyone that was on the playground that day. He pressed his thumbs into either side of his neck for several seconds, thereby cutting off the blood supply to his brain. He collapsed to the ground, flailing around like he was having a fit, which of course the audience found hilarious.

With our, "Monkey see, monkey do," philosophy of the day, several of the other children started their own experiments. Stubby, he of bulging eyes, was there in a flash and put a stop to it, lickety-split. I believe all classes were spoken to that day about the danger of the behaviour.

. . .

What can it mean
You're just a summer's dream

Summer soon came. Sunny days would find us at nearby Sunderland Lake. By no means were sunny summer days as warm as they are now, but the village kids flocked to the lake just the same.

Sunderland Lake is large . . . about 16 kilometres long, and can be as deep as 200 metres in places. It is notoriously cold but crystal clear. Some say it is so cold that no algae or other form of plant life can survive in it. Certainly, if one looked across and down the lake, large areas of snow could be seen trailing down mountainsides to the water, even during the peak of summer.

One May, which was far too early to be swimming, I dove into the lake after a "dare," and regretted it immediately. It was so COLD. I developed an instant headache. But during the summer months, we youngsters could handle the still-chilly lake. It warmed up for about a week in late August, if fall rains hadn't come early.

Typically, we'd meet on bikes over in front of Buzz and Gumpers' place—and wait. They were usually late, not so much being challenged to organize themselves to get a swimsuit and towel, but because they'd not finished a chore that had to be done before being granted leave for the day.

Off we'd go. A caravan of five to eight bikes, the number varying depending on how many boys might be grounded by their parents on that particular day. Down past the entrance to Camp, down to the old railway right of way. We'd turn right and for the first kilometre or so of the five-kilometre journey, have the old rough, gravel railway bed to contend with. This was the slower part of the ride. It could be tough on the backside. Those bikes back in the sixties had neither forgiving alloy frames nor any kind of a suspension.

On one occasion, Gumper, who was leading the caravan, dismounted from his bike and disappeared into the bush. Reappearing a few seconds later with a length of abandoned garden hose rolled up and thrown over his shoulder, and with an "I need this for something," he remounted and we were off again.

We bugged Gumper the whole way to the lake, hoping he'd reveal what his plan was, because he often had a plan that resulted in some good entertainment. Finally arriving at the lake, we parked our bikes (no need for locks back then) and spread our towels in a row on the lakeshore. We tested the water temperature with our toes, which was pretty much the definition of over optimism because it was always cold.

The swimming and beach area in those days was known as the Point. A long line of huge logs (booms), connected end to end by large chains, delineated the swimming area. From the beach, there was a line of logs heading straight out to a raft. These logs were big enough to easily provide a dry way to get to the raft if you had decent balance. Although they could vibrate or roll at times in response to waves from a boat that passed by outside the border booms or by someone intentionally trying to move them.

Another potential obstacle to getting to the raft dry was when someone challenged you on a boom. Face to face, we'd reach our arms out to grasp hands with our opponent. After a brief tussle, one or both combatants would be tossed into the cold, cold, lake. Ahh, the vivid memory of the scream a kid could produce when hitting the water for the first dip of the day.

On this particular day, our gang kind of lagged behind on the shore, waiting to see what Gumper's plans were for the hose. With it over his shoulder, he jumped onto the first boom and easily moved along from there, boom to boom, until he got to the raft. We followed until all of us . . . Deano, Buzz, Chunk, Turnip, Calvin, and me were on the raft as well, waiting for "showtime."

"You guys gotta see this," exclaimed Gumper. "I'll bet you've never seen anything like it!"

With that he unrolled the hose and passed one end to his brother.

"Buzz, you hold this end of the hose outta the water—no matter what."

With that, he put his own hand flat over the other end of the hose to prevent water from getting in and jumped off the raft. Unfortunately, Gumper had underestimated his buoyancy. He wasn't going be able to demonstrate his long, "snorkel," because whenever he tried to get under the surface of the water, he floated back up. I wouldn't have thought a bone rack like Gump would float.

He rejoined us on the raft, and almost immediately announced that he had another idea. He and Buzz ran the booms back to shore. My other friends and I settled into the good life of lying on the raft, and soaking up the sun.

Awhile later, the brothers returned. Scavenging in the woods, Gumper and Buzz had found a piece of nylon rope and a large flat rock just the weight to sink Gumper.

Gumper held the rock to his tummy while Buzz went round and round his belly with the rope, finally knotting it off. The commencement procedure was then repeated. Buzz got his directions again to hold one end of the hose out of the water. Gumper flattened his hand and held it firmly over the other end. Then he jumped off the raft.

It took a moment or two for the bubbles to clear and, thanks to the crystal clear water, my friends and I could see everything as we hung our heads over the edge of the raft. Gumper completed his descent to the bottom of the lake. I'd estimate at that point the lake was three-and-one-half to four-and-one-half metres deep. I'd made it to the bottom before on a dare but boy did my ears hurt when I reached it.

For Act One, Gumper had us laughing our heads off. He strutted around on the bottom like he was a fine English gentleman out for a walk.

Act Two commenced when Gump couldn't hold his breath any longer. We saw the bubbles from his exhalation. Then he brought the end of the hose up to his mouth, removed his hand covering the opening, locked his lips on the end of the hose and inhaled. Now I don't know what law of physics is at play when one tries to suck air through a six-metre long hose, or whether the hose was obstructed by dirt or a dead mouse, which Gump later hypothesized because the hose end tasted funny, but Gumper couldn't get any air. And boy did he try. Which of course looked absolutely hilarious to us.

For the final act, he threw down the end of the hose and began procedures to abort the mission. He frantically tried to swim upwards but the rock was too heavy and the rope had been too well-knotted by Buzz. Despite how hard he pushed off with his legs, he couldn't get farther than about half a metre off the lake floor, and then he'd sink back down. This was better than any slapstick movie. He then tried to suck in what little tummy he had and furiously wiggled to dislodge the rock. Finally . . . finally . . . the rock slid to the bottom and Gumper shot to and through the surface of the lake like an underwater ballistic missile. We dragged him up on to the raft and slapped him on the back. Gump had delivered yet again. At the time I don't think it crossed any of our minds just how dangerous the stunt had been.

XX

"If you're horrible to me, I'm going to write a song about it, and you won't like it. That's how I operate."

—*Taylor Swift*

If ever there was a stereotype of a bully, Chubby Paulsen was it. Two or three years older, he might not have been twice our size, although he was considerably taller, but he was twice our weight. Luckily, Chubby lived down towards Alston so typically we didn't encounter him up in Sunderland very often.

But . . . he did frequent the lake in the summertime. Many times I wondered why, oh why, would someone that huge want to expose the mountain of flesh that he was at a public beach. I don't know. To be fair, my friends and I weren't going to win any body-building championships at that point, either. Think of one of those large, four-litre Javex bleach containers. The circumference of our chests wasn't much bigger.

If Chubby Paulsen could make your life miserable, he would. If you were lying on a beach towel, he'd dump water on you. If you were standing near the water, you'd be pushed in. If you were on the raft and he happened to be there . . .

One day, Chubby was doing his regular clean-off of the raft. He'd grab an innocent kid, who was likely stretched out and drying off in the sunshine, swing him by the arm so that with all the force his largeness could create, the kid would go flying into the air before landing in the lake. One by one, Chubby would toss them in. When few remained, you'd try to dodge him. But sooner rather than later he'd corner you and have you by the arm. Seconds later, off you went.

On this particular day, Chubby had cleared the raft except for two kids—me and Buzz. We were tripping over one another as we tried to avoid him but he got a hold of Buzz's arm. Leading him over to the edge of the raft, he swung him. Seconds after, Buzz went flying into the air, and just seconds after that, I did something that made me, "Hero of the Day."

I can't say a lot of thought went into it. I was known for my impulsivity. I ran across the raft and threw my spindly body at Chubby, connecting with him at about the level of his hips. Like a gigantic skin bag of jelly, his body shook as he tried to regain his balance . . . but he couldn't. Waving both arms wildly, he went off the edge of the raft and into the water. The kids in the water cheered. The people on the beach cheered. I stood triumphantly on the raft and bathed in the adulation.

"You're dead, Moore," shouted Chubby.

I decided I'd had enough swimming for the day. Perhaps it was a good time to head home. I dove in, did my fastest crawl to the beach, and was on my bike in seconds.

. . .

In the 1960s three resource-based industries dominated British Columbia's economy: forestry, mining and fishing. Fifty cents out of every dollar came out of forestry. In the village at that time, the coal-mining industry was over and people had by and large transitioned to forestry.

I heard it said many times that most of Sunderland had been mined underneath. I always thought it peculiar that the villagers spoke of this as if it were something to be proud of. I'd had the thought that my bicycle and I would disappear into some huge sinkhole, particularly if I happened to be riding on coal slag found in many places around the village.

Not far from the Point was a boomed off area where hundreds of big logs floated, awaiting a time when they would be pulled across the lake to a log sort/loading area. In fact, you could walk along one single stretch of booms from the raft all the way to this football field sized area of logs. Which is what we would do.

We knew this was a dangerous area, despite our pre-teen sense of invulnerability. Once there, we'd run along the tops of logs, some about 30 centimetres in diameter, these ones sunk a bit as your weight landed on them. There were also some behemoth monsters, about a metre in diameter. These were old-growth trees.

If you happened to fall on your jaunt, you could bang your knees up on a log quite badly, or worse yet, fall into a gap between the logs and be submerged. In which case the logs tended to move back together. You had to stay calm to push them apart so that your head could break the surface, get some air, and you could haul yourself up onto a log.

On a certain day of running the logs, we came across a log that was standing on end. It was a big one, about one-and-a-half metres in diameter. About 60 centimetres of it stuck out of the water, and I'd estimate another four metres was submerged. For some reason, Gumper climbed on top of it. It started to move downward. Following Gumper's instructions, another two or three of us climbed on. The log started to go down. We crouched and held on to the rough edge of the log. Down we went, under the water for about a metre and a half, until the other end of the log hit bottom.

We swam off to the sides and up it went, eventually shooting out of the water well over a metre.

"It's a Zomper," declared Gumper. And a new game was born.

Four of us would climb on the end and grab on. Down the log would go. When we hit bottom, everyone would swim off to the sides, except one designated daredevil. The log would go up and the lucky guy would get a good ride up through the water's surface and into the air about a metre. What fun!

We all took turns, until one time everyone peeled off the log underwater and swam off to the sides. I don't know what Buzz was doing but somehow he ended up swimming above the log as it made its journey upward. I think Buzz was still swimming as he was taken, fully stretched out on the top of the log as it shot out of the water, with a look of terror on his face. We laughed and laughed about it until the reality set in of just how dangerous this new game was. What if a log had floated above Buzz and the Zomper? He surely would have been crushed.

. . .

Some days, one group of my friends were off to the lake, while a couple of my other friends would be riding their bikes down to Alston for a day of fishing in the "salt chuck." "Chuck" meant "water" in the near extinct indigenous Chinook language, so salt chuck referred to saltwater, that is, the ocean.

Bowser, reddish haired and freckle-faced, was head fisher. It was a habit of mine to closely examine Bowser's face as the summer progressed to take inventory of how much the freckles had grown in size due to the sunshine. I had a theory that if we had a sunny summer and Bowser stayed in the sun long enough, all the freckles would merge together and Bowser would have a darker face.

Somehow Bowser convinced Foo, he of tall and skinny physical proportions, that there was good fishing off the dock. It was a long bike ride to get to Alston, more than six kilometres—mind you it was mostly downhill once you got past the "Whoopsie-daisies." The Whoopsie-daisies were a couple of hills just outside of town on the Alston road, separated by quite a dip between them. On a bike they were a challenge. In a car, well, as kids we loved the feeling as the tires almost left the ground after peaking each hill.

The ride back by bike was brutal. I think I joined them on one fishing trip and, on that occasion, borrowed a dime off Foo to phone my mum, pleading for her to come pick me up.

(Somehow those long torturous bike rides stayed with Foo. He became an avid road cyclist and competed throughout the Lower Mainland. The guy is still riding! He told me awhile back he joined a practise ride with a bunch of young guys on a ride to Tsawwassen from Burnaby. The two-hour ride out wasn't bad; between drafting the younger riders, and a decent tailwind, he kept up. On the ride back, however, there was a headwind. He was dropped by the pack and rode for four hours by himself to get home. Silly old git. Act your age!)

Honestly, I couldn't get into Bowser's idea of big-game fishing. Sitting on a rough wood dock and suffering sliver after sliver into the back of my thighs wasn't my idea of fun, even if periodically one of us would land a monster 15-centimetre-long bullhead. I was better-suited to risking my life every day hanging out at the lake with Gumper and Buzz.

Those fish weren't good for anything other than an exclamation from Foo, "God, these fish are ugly," which he would utter several times during the course of the proceedings. Once they were reeled in and unhooked, back they went into the salt chuck. I don't know how many times those guys caught the same fish over their summer of fish love, but I suspect it was many.

Foo recounted to me how Bowser hatched a plan that changed one routine outing. Bowser searched the seashore for a small piece of wood that looked to be a good floater. Once seated on the end of the dock, he baited his hook with a big piece of bacon. Dropping his floater into the water, he lowered his baited hook onto the floater and let out a lot of fishing line from his reel.

Foo said it happened fast. A seagull swooped down, swallowed the bacon and hook, and took off. He got a ways but then the slack was taken up on Bowser's reel. The seagull's flight was over.

. . .

The salt chuck had much more interesting wildlife than the lake ever did, and we got to see it up close when my dad bought a boat off Mustang Monteith, who later became mayor of Sunderland and one of British Columbia's longest-serving mayors. Mustang built the boat with his own hands. The 17-foot *MarCee* was equipped with a 45-horse Johnson outboard motor, which was a huge motor, at least in physical dimensions back in the day. There were trips to Tree Island and Hornby Island, salmon fishing adventures (many useless dogfish were caught), sightings of blackfish, and the occasional anxious moment when the sea got choppy.

The adults even got to waterski. I always found it boring waiting for a newbie to get the hang of it. One time, Addie Harston, a good friend of the family who had babysat Calvin and me when we were little tots, came along to give it a go. She was having a heck of a time and feeling increasingly embarrassed. I'm sure it didn't help much when I shouted out, "Addie, get your big fat bum off the water."

Mum and Dad liked to take visiting prairie relatives out on the boat. Most of them were very nervous since they didn't know how to swim. Dad explained that there weren't many lakes around where he had grown up and those that were close by were not very suitable for swimming. I, in fact, can confirm that. When I was 13 years old, I visited my Auntie Rose and my very elderly grandmother in Minnedosa, Manitoba. On a hot summer's day, my cousins took me to the lake (it looked like a pond). I ran to the end of the dock and jumped. Opening my eyes underwater I couldn't see a thing other than green, and I could feel the slime of algae all over my skin. Ugh! A sharp contrast to the crystal-clear water of the rivers and lakes I'd grown up with.

The prairie relatives were fascinated by the large, purple star-fish that stuck on the undersides of gigantic rocks near the boat launch site. Unknown to my family, one relative gathered a whole bunch of them up, put them in a plastic bag, and stuffed them into their car's trunk. Hoping, I guess, to impress their friends back in Manitoba with the beautiful creatures. We heard that starfish don't look or smell too good after storage in a car trunk for three hot summer days.

XXI

A regular "go to" for entertainment purposes when your parents weren't around was to gather around the wall-mounted kitchen phone with a friend or two and make a gag phone call. There were different variations:

There was the standard one-man technique:

"Hello, does your roof leak?"
"Why, no."
"Well, how did a big drip like you get in?"

The tag-team technique:
Stuey: "Hello, is George there?"
Victim: "There's no George here. You must have the wrong number."
Stuey: "Oh, okay, sorry to bother you."
Then a few minutes later, Cale would phone the same number:
Cale: "Hello, could I speak to George, please?"
Victim: "There's no George here."
Cale: "Oh, sorry."
Finally, I would phone the same number yet again and in a different voice say:
"Hello, this is George. Were there any calls for me?"

Oh, those wonderful days before call display existed!
My favourite of all was a call to the butcher shop:
"Hello, do you have pig's feet?"
"Yes."
"Well, put shoes on and nobody will know."

. . .

Our house had two telephones! People were impressed. There was the beige wall-mounted phone in the kitchen and a black desktop phone that sat on my father's bedside table, necessary for night-time emergency calls. We must have had muscles back in the day, since the receivers themselves were quite heavy. The black phone on my dad's bedside table could certainly inflict a concussion, or worse, if it had ever been thrown at someone's head, like I'd seen in the movies.

Sometimes, I'd sneak upstairs to my father's phone, pick up the receiver, dial nine, and then our phone number, pause, then hang up. Seconds later, both household phones would ring. I'd wait a few rings and then pickup to hear my mother say, "Hello, Moore residence."

I'd respond with something endearing like, "What's for dinner, Mum?"

Ha! When I was well into puberty and my voice had changed I could be mistaken for my father when I answered the phone.

"Hello," I said, answering the ringing phone.

"Dr. Moore, this is Boris Stafford. My wife has a growth of some kind on her backside," said a panicked voice on the other end of the line.

"Oh, just a minute, I'll get my dad."

Even though I was curious, I knew enough not to ask my dad in the days following, "How is Mrs. Stafford's bum?"

. . .

The sixties were a huge takeoff time for technology. We didn't realize it at the time. Battery-operated toys started popping up, colour TVs replaced the old black and whites, and tape recorders became readily available to the average consumer.

Calvin received a tape recorder for his birthday one year. I was totally jealous. It was portable and battery-operated. It was sweet! At the time, Cal had pretty much moved past his infatuation with monsters like the werewolf, the creature of the black lagoon, and Frankenstein, although he still had several properly assembled and wonderfully painted models of them in his room. Oh, and to complete the picture of a brother who went through a stage of having morbid interests, he had great interest in shows like, *The Outer Limits*, and later, *The Twilight Zone*. Programs that would freak me out.

Cal developed an interest in the prehistoric world. I distinctly remember he recorded the sound from a National Geographic TV special with Dr. Leakey, detailing an archaeological dig in Africa. I know he listened to it many times. While the monotone voice of Dr. Leakey didn't interest me, it obviously inspired Calvin because eventually he went off to university to study archaeology, and farther down the road spend time working at the National Museum of Tanzania, going on early man digs. He even experienced a bout of malaria! Quite a world away from the little village of Sunderland.

As a teenager, Cal brought his tape recorder along when the entire family accompanied my dad to St. Lucia, a Caribbean island, for a one month's physician volunteer assignment. It was an awesome trip . . . more in the next bestseller. Suffice it to say, we were the only white family and outsiders in a town called Dennery.

Cal introduced his technology to a St. Lucian kid one day. He'd pre-recorded the following on his tape recorder, "Two (pause),

Four (pause), Six." When the kid dropped around to our govern-ment-provided house one afternoon, Cal did some education.

"This is a computer," said Cal. "It can answer any question you want. Watch this. What is one plus one?"

Cal pushed the Play button. "Two," spoke the tape recorder. Then he pushed Stop.

The kid looked puzzled.

"What is two plus two?" Cal pushed play.

"Four," said the tape recorder. After which Cal pushed stop.

At this point, the kid had a very puzzled look on his face and his eyes flittered back and forth from the machine to Cal.

"What is three plus three?" Again Cal pushed play.

"Six," answered the tape recorder.

"Now," said Calvin, with somewhat of an air of superiority, "What do you think of my computer?"

The boy replied. "In my country we call this a tape recorder."

XXII

The other day I was watching a classic hockey game on the Sports Network featuring the Montreal Canadiens versus the Toronto Maple Leafs. It's really difficult not to become overcome with sentiment at these times. The greats: Jean Beliveau, Bobby Baun, Davey Keon, Frank Mahovlich skating up and down the ice, throwing hits, in black and white. Even if there was the need for some imagination since I could barely see the puck.

Some of my memories have begun to fade to grey as well. It is impossible for me to access colour in the following story.

It was well before Lena was born. I must have been three years old. We had taken the long journey to Vancouver to visit friends and do some shopping at Eaton's department store. There was a confusing array of different departments, spread out on several floors, separated by escalators. I'd never seen anything like it. The store dwarfed Clifton's Eaton's, that's for sure.

Cal must have been with my dad . . . likely in the shoe department because shoes were my dad's thing. He always said that he couldn't find shoes in Sunderland or Clifton because his feet were too big. I think the explanation for his attraction to big-city shoe departments had a lot to do with his childhood. Growing up in the Depression in rural Manitoba with big feet and six older brothers meant he had always inherited worn shoes that didn't fit. The end result was that dad always placed special value on his footwear. He was always on the lookout for new shoes, despite having quite a collection already. I knew because I could spend an afternoon in his well-organized closet trying them all on, and leaving the closet not so well-organized!

Anyway, somehow I'd drawn my mum on this particular day. We wandered around displays of towels, sheets, and pillows. All the while I did what I had been told, which was to hold on to my mom's black jacket sleeve, near the cuff. Temporarily, I must have let go of my mum's sleeve. I recall we were moving again, and I had a good hold on a black sleeve, when a woman looked down at me and said, "Who are you, little boy?" I looked from her cuff to her face, confused. This wasn't my mother.

I started to cry. The woman consoled me the best she could but I really wanted my mother back, even if it meant spending more time looking at towels. She led me to the cashier. An announcement was made:

"Ladies and Gentleman, we have a lost boy. He says his name is Stuey. He is about three years old and he is very unhappy. He has lost his mother. Could she please come to the checkout counter in the home section of the store?"

Happily, I was soon reunited with my mum. I remember the big hug, and then I was instructed to hold onto her sleeve. Off we went again, shopping.

I am the custodian of two photos which I'm sure were taken on West Georgia or Granville St, Vancouver, by one of those sidewalk photographers that would jump out, take a photograph, and then try to sell it to you. In the first photo, my father is carrying Calvin. Cal looks calm. Dad looks a little rushed. I can tell by his long stride which is captured in the photo. In the second photo, my mother is carrying me. She looks cross. By my contorted body and the way my mother is holding me I can surmise I am squirming. I do not look at all happy either.

. . .

My mum and sister must have been away on another trip to the big city because one Sunday night my father announced that the three men of the family were going to go out for dinner in the city of Clifton.

My brother and I were relieved. Our last experience with my father's cooking had involved a strange concoction that he called tomato soup. Picture big blobs of stewed tomatoes floating in a milk and buttery mixture. Somehow my brother had managed to eat part of his and thereby had been granted the greatly prized, "excused from the table." I, on the other hand, couldn't stomach it. My, "I protesteth loudly" and hereby "refusedth to eateth," did not go over. I think I was detained for 30 minutes before my father recognized my resolve, and/or he'd sampled his cooking and concluded it was not going to win any awards.

We jumped in the red Beetle and off we went to Clifton. I think we stopped by Mr. Mike's first, home of the famous Mike Burger. Cal steadfastly maintained that the regular Mike Burger could not compete with the Mike Burger *with cheese*. Unfortunately, I could not test his premise. Mr. Mike's was closed. On we went from there to several other establishments before concluding that in the future people would surely be better off if restaurants were open on Sundays.

Home we went. I don't recall what was on the menu but for sure it wasn't tomato soup. I would have remembered that.

XXIII

Jamie Renzo. A ha! I now summon my quest for revenge, which has been repressed for years.

Jamie was Cale's brother. Three years older than Cale and I, he was most often a bane to our existence. He was like Eddie Haskell from the TV show *Leave It To Beaver*. Why, he could even ruin my journey to paradise whenever I happened to dine over at the Renzo's house, particularly when Mrs. Renzo made her Yorkshire pudding (I think I concluded there was something wrong with my mother because she couldn't duplicate Mrs. Renzo's. Mum's would always flop over and be kind of mushy inside. They were edible if you smothered them with gravy, but they were like a two or three, while Mrs. Renzo's were a 10).

Many a time, prematurely white-haired Mr. Renzo would bark, "Leave them alone, Jamie!" If Jamie could pester us in front of his parents', in the Renzo's cosy little house, imagine what he could accomplish when not adequately supervised.

Cale and I were practising our mastery of doubling on my bike on Bellemont Street, next to Moore's Forest, when Jamie came along and proposed that we do a triple. Hmm. I think Cale and I both felt a similar twinge of anxiety, which often accompanied engagement with Jamie; it would be more prudent to run the other way.

Against my better judgment, I climbed on to the handlebars, while Jamie held the bike. Cale climbed up on to the seat. Jamie slid his leg over the bar and pushed us off. Away we went. Wow! Three on a bike! Jamie had come up with a great idea! But then we went faster and faster as Jamie peddled down the hill. Seated on the handlebars with nothing in front of me, my panic rose. Suddenly, somehow Jamie lost control. The handlebars shifted to one side and we crashed. We went down hard. No broken bones but definitely scrapes and bruises. There were tears from Cale and me.

Another day brought a problem that I was having with a rope that hung from a tree located beside our home's garage. I had ascertained it would be a perfect rope swing, but the bottom of the rope had this huge knot which was, I don't know why, an obstacle. Suddenly, Jamie appeared. Likely he had been having a puff in Moore's Forest and had seen the opportunity to be of assistance.

He suggested we cut the huge knot off. I agreed it was necessary to do so.

"How do we do it?" I asked Jamie.

"It's easy," replied Jamie. "Have you got an axe?"

I ran to the basement and returned with an axe.

"What now?

"Simple," said Jamie, "You hold the rope against the tree and I'll chop the knot off."

"You'll get my finger."

"Don't worry," Jamie reassured me, "I'm good with an axe."

I held the rope against the tree with my right index finger.

Jamie swung the axe. The axe head landed almost exactly in the centre of my fingernail, instantly and amazingly splitting it right in half. Blood squirted. I retreated to my house for first aid. My finger survived, but in a few days both sides of the nail fell off. For a while I had a nail-less finger with which to scare the girls.

. . .

Herman's Hermits. The Renzos had a portable record player with just the one fabric-covered speaker on the front. Its volume couldn't be cranked up too loud because the sound would start to distort, not to mention that Mrs. Renzo wouldn't be too happy with Cale and me, particularly because we played the same 45 RPM record over and over: *Henry the Eighth*. I thought it strange that the widow had been married seven times before.

After playing the record a time or two, Cale and I would lend our voices to it. It wouldn't be long before Mrs. Renzo suggested we play out in the backyard, "But don't go in the shed."

As was a common occurrence, once we got to having a good time playing, Jamie appeared. He had a large, what looked to be empty, Heinz pickle jar. You know the ones: they're about 20 centimetres in length and have a tin screw-top lid.

"I've got something to show you guys and you're not going to believe it," said Jamie excitedly. Which, in retrospect, should have been our first warning sign that, "Jamie, gonna be Jamie."

"It's really hard to see," he continued. "Unscrew the top and look really quick in the bottom."

He handed the jar to me. I guess as privileged guest at the Renzo home, Jamie was giving me first try.

I can do that, I thought.

I unscrewed the lid carefully and removed it, moving the jar closer to my eyes. I couldn't see anything in the bottom of the jar.

"No, closer, you moron," coached Jamie.

With my eyes transfixed on the inside bottom of the jar, I moved my face so close to the jar opening that my eyebrows touched the rim and my nose was pretty much inserted into the jar.

"Yick," I shouted, as my entire body recoiled from the jar. The putrid smell causing my body to react involuntarily. What malodorous form of a trick was this?

After he picked himself up off the grass, from whence he had been rolling around with unrestrained laughter, Jamie explained.

It was a fart in a jar.

XIV

I didn't much know Ticky Baylor.

How he got to be called, "Ticky," I don't know. Possibly he had a tic or two, a manifestation of the neurological condition of Tourette's Syndrome. Or perhaps the name was reflective of his tendency to blow up like a bomb after repeated bullying (tick, tick, tick . . .).

I recall seeing a T-shirt a number of years ago entitled, "Nicknames of Sunderland." Just about everyone I knew had a nickname when I was growing up. Heck, I knew some people very well, but never did know their Christian name. Luckily, Calvin and I escaped having nicknames for most of our pre-adolescence. But when Cal filled out to be a big boy with a beard and long scruffy hair, he was aptly named "Grizzly." By virtue of being Grizzly's younger brother, I became "Bear." However, neither of our nicknames stuck.

For a while, I assumed there was someone over at the village office that was in charge of assigning nicknames. I thought, *Hmm . . . that could be an interesting job.*

Anyhow . . . back to Ticky. My buddies and I had a plan to check out Chinese Creek. Someone had told me that they'd seen some good-sized trout in one of the larger creek's pools. I walked up to the New Houses and met a couple of friends. As we were walking towards Hillmont Road, about to descent it down to the old railroad grade, there was Ticky, standing by a stop sign, kicking rocks.

It just struck me. What a great name for a novel or a movie: "Kicking Rocks." I mean, yeah, obviously one would have to think of some other ideas other than Ticky standing by a stop sign, kicking rocks.

Without invitation, Ticky managed to attach himself to our caravan and immediately started showing us his new jacket, going on about it at length. I think we managed to get a few words in edgewise once we got down to the railway grade but then he started up about it again. In retrospect, I can imagine that getting a new jacket was a very big deal for some kids when their families were nearly living in poverty. But, of course, at the time Ticky was just being downright annoying, going on and on about his jacket.

In a short while, we turned left off the railway grade and walked down what was once the great main street of Chinatown. At one time more than 2,000 people inhabited this part of Sunderland, but at this time in history there was nothing left of it. A kilometre further and we came to Chinese Creek, that oasis of crystal clear water. We spent a couple of hours walking along the creek banks, spotting some trout that enticed us to plan a fishing trip in the near future.

As we were leaving the creek, Ticky started complaining that his stomach was bothering him. I don't know what form of gastric distress he was in but he disappeared into the bush, hollering, "Wait for me guys; I'll just be a sec."

We heard him shouting curse words a minute or two later. Shortly thereafter he appeared, holding his jacket as far away from his nose as he could. Turns out that Ticky had been in such a hurry to do his business, he'd: found a suitable spot, threw off his jacket, did his business, then realized the sin he'd committed.

Once we got over the laugh of the day, I think we all felt very badly for Ticky, but that didn't stop us from demanding that he, jacket in outstretched hand, walk 20 or so paces behind us as we made our way back to town.

Note to Ticky: Ticky, I don't know what ever became of you. I suppose you could be hopping mad at me for telling the story. You might even want to consider legal action. I'm just letting you know that I already consulted a lawyer. He said you've got no legal case. "Defecation of Character," is not in the legal statutes.

. . .

For all the bullying that Ticky and, by association, his family endured (and I'm confident there was much), there was a day I shall never forget where all voices were silenced, except one Baylor child. I can't recall the event. It must have been a performance of some kind that came to the SRI hall, for it was packed full of many of the village's populace. At some point members of the audience were invited to hold the microphone and tell a story or sing a song. There were many giggles as stagestruck villagers couldn't find their words when staring down the end of the microphone.

People were already mumbling to one another and laughing as Ticky's little sister, Josie, got closer and closer to the front of the line to take a turn. "Oh, this will be good," said someone close by, tongue in cheek.

The ambient noise dropped a notch as Josie, who was about a metre tall and nine years old, was handed the microphone. She began. I will never forget the sound that came out of that little girl's mouth, or how she calmly looked around the room at the people who were tuned in to find something to criticize. . . something that would be fodder to bully Ticky with. There wasn't a noise to be heard as she sang so clearly, so in tune, so strongly that the sound filled the hall:

A cloud can change the day
Make the sunshine seem so far away
The weather has to change
But my love will stay the same
My love will stay the same.

XXV

Sublime. That is the word I would use to describe the red Honda Trail 50 that came to be ours when my brother and I were in the late stages of our childhood. I don't know how it came about. I suspect maybe Calvin had advocated for it with Dad. Maxie Dougwell had a trail bike. It made sense for Cal to have one to follow Maxie around on. At any rate, it was a gift from the Gods.

It had those short fat tires that offered much stability, and a three-speed, automatic-clutch transmission. First gear got you up to about the speed of a power-driven lawnmower. Top speed was about 45 kilometres per hour. It was not going to challenge a Triumph Bonneville, but a 12-year-old kid could have a lot of fun on it.

Initially, we were confined to riding it in our yard but, eventually, after Cal and I had ground a significant big circle into the lower lawn, dad relented and gave us permission to explore. We'd scoot up the sidewalk past the Di Caro's, make a sharp left at the junior-high entrance, scoot along a trail beside the top field, and shortly be on the gravelled Number Five Mine road. Freedom. From there you could bomb out to the dump, maybe get lucky and chase a bear over the coal slag, or drive on to the lake over old mining or logging roads. The world was our oyster!

I can remember following a logging road up a mountain on the south side of the lake. In my young brain, I was starting to think that just a little further on I could descend into Port Hibernia. I'd heard that some village politicians were advocating for an over the mountains highway to that village, which was located at the head of an inlet that connected to Vancouver Island's West Coast. Their case was that it could easily be done since there were rough, in some cases abandoned logging roads that already connected Sunderland to Port Hibernia.

But when I looked down to my right, way, way down was Sunderland Lake. I was obviously not as far along as I'd imagined.

On another logging road adventure, I made an ill-advised decision to goose the throttle and drive into a huge pothole that was filled with water. As the bike slipped out from underneath me, I flicked the kill switch with my thumb. I was left standing in a puddle about 50 centimetres deep with no bike to be seen. Once I found it and got it out of the puddle (no easy task), she started right up.

Another time I got a flat rear tire way out in the backcountry. The bike was impossible to push home with that fat flat tire. I had a two-hour walk to get home. Mum and I creeped along some rough logging roads with the truck to retrieve the bike. We dropped it off for a patch job at Bill Petit's Gulf Station on our way home. Cal would have to wait another day for his turn with the bike.

It's true. It pretty much worked like that. One brother would return home with a near empty tank of gas. The other would be waiting to fill 'er up and take his turn. For a while, we felt we were the luckiest kids in the whole village. It wasn't long before some other kids got bikes. I remember Jack Walston got a Honda 70. We were jealous! His bike had an extra gear and a higher top speed. Somehow Bowser got an old Suzuki street bike. It smoked, had narrow tires that made the bike a challenge to handle in gravel, and its shocks would bottom out on bumpy roads. I'm pretty sure that Bowser, however, would report he loved his bike as much as we loved ours.

. . .

I've had the same dream for years. I'm in the basement of the old house snooping around. Over in a corner by the workshop, there's a tarp covering something. I walk over to it and give the tarp a tug. Off it comes, revealing the Honda SL100 that Cal and I grew into after the Honda 50.

I throw my leg over, lift the kickstand with my left foot, turn the petcock valve, pull out the choke, reach down, ready the kickstart leg, and push down. She starts.

. . .

"The Dump"

The dump was definitely a popular destination both in pre- and post- trail bike times. In those days, it consisted of a long hilltop of coal slag. There was no gated fancy-dancy recycling factory back then. You just drove out onto the flat strip and threw your garbage over either side, trying to get it to roll the nine or so metres to the bottom.

When Calvin and Maxie Dougwell weren't down at the Home Store buying fudgsicles, they used to drive out to the dump in the evenings. They'd stop in the middle of the strip, shut the car down, and wait. In a while, bears would come scavenging through the garbage. Maxie would simultaneously flick his lights on as he started the car and proceed to chase a bear until the bear went tumbling over the bank.

Yes, in those days there were no fees, no weigh scale, no check-in station, no, "Where are you coming from today, sir?"

"Panama. I drove all the way up here just to dump my garbage and pay outta the nose for it."

Of course when you stop at the station on your way out these days you do indeed, pay through the nose for it!

Back in the day there was just one piece of machinery, a bulldozer, which was driven by Bennie the Bump. Bennie would fire up the dozer every once and a while and push garbage over the banks. Even I could see that it must have been a boring job. But . . . there were perks!

It was amazing what could get dropped off at the dump. It was always worth a good poke around to see what you could find. Heck, I used to park the trail bike at one end and walk along the strip, looking for treasures.

Once when I was 16, Mum sent me to the dump with a truckload of household garbage. As I was unloading the truck. I noticed that there was a flurry of activity from a group of men standing around a good-sized pile. As I got closer, I realized the pile, more than a metre high and two metres wide, consisted of bundles of magazines. The men were breaking the straps holding the bundles together and cracking the mags open. I was thinking maybe they were *National Geographic* or *Popular Science*. Turns out they were adult magazines! It was like Christmas morning, your birthday, and a solar eclipse — all rolled into one! I managed to get more than my fair share.

XXVI

As to be expected, we were granted more independence as we got to the cusp of our teenage years. And the new freedom could have resulted in trouble or tragedy.

With the construction of the new junior-high school up by the top field, we discovered a whole new play area. It was fascinating to watch the structure take shape. The gymnasium went up fast. To us, a group of five or six of us, mostly kids from the New Houses, it was the most impressive feature of the new school since it was the tallest. As it was going up we would climb it every few days happy to discover that a new challenge in scaling it existed, often treacherously scampering up scaffolding leaning against a wall. Eventually, the roof was completed. We marvelled at the view and revelled in the thrill of being at such a height.

It was Billy Montrose, Greig's older brother, who came up with the idea. There were large pieces of heavy-duty plastic spread around on parts of the roof. Billy took a large piece, grabbed two corners in each hand, approached the edge of the three-storey-high building, and jumped! It was amazing. The plastic billowed and acted like a parachute. Before long, we were taking turns. I don't know how someone didn't get hurt that evening.

In a year or so the school was up and running. I was still in elementary school but I was in the school one evening, albeit in a unauthorized manner.

A bunch of my friends and I joined up one evening with a group of teenage boys, headed up by Larry Peterson's older brother, Wes. He had reputedly been in trouble with the law. We walked down the old Number Five Mine road a ways, and then followed Wes into the bush . . . to his lair. He'd done a decent job of making a small, rudimentary log cabin, although there were big cracks between the small trees he'd used to construct it. Still, we thought it was pretty cool.

The plan for the evening was soon revealed. We were going to break into the school. I didn't think it was a great idea, but I couldn't speak up against the older boys. Apparently, Wes had been in the school a few times already. There was a window in a room, which later became my French classroom, that didn't close properly. It could easily be slid open.

Off to the school we went. Wes slid open the window. One by one each of us climbed up and through the window. It was dark. We were instructed not to turn on a light. Wes led us down a short hallway, then we took a left down a longer hallway, then a right towards the gym. But before we got there Wes stopped us, crossed the hallway, opened a door, and ushered us into a small room that contained some counters, cabinets, and a fridge. It was the school's canteen. Within seconds, we each had a pop and at least one bag of chips or cheesies.

Wes knew how to run an operation. He had us out of the building in about three minutes.

That was my last "break and enter." My conscience bothered me.

. . .

Foo, Chunk, and I used to hitchhike into Clifton from time to time on a weekend night. Our destination was always the Clifton movie theatre. In those days no one worried about thumbing a ride. Most often you knew the person that pulled over for you.

We knew to expect, "Where are you boys off to? I bet you're going to the movies."

I don't recall what movie we saw on that particular night. It might have been *Sabata, The Guns of The Magnificent Seven, Planet of the Apes*, or *Where Eagles Dare* . . . but the best show of all occurred on our way home.

We walked under street lights up the main drag from the theatre, turned left on Ireland Ave, and had just turned right onto Sunderland Road, our favourite hitchhiking spot, when Chunk said, "Stop guys—look!"

Directly in front of us, not seven metres away, was a large window in which a topless woman stood. She appeared to be washing dishes. We must have stood there for 10 minutes, not so much concentrating on the plates she'd move from the sink to the drying rack every few seconds. With our mouths open in amazement, we thanked the gods for the gift.

. . .

If there were challenges with group composition in elementary school, imagine what junior high school brought when, increasingly, testosterone reared its ugly head.

I don't know if it was some kind of sophisticated social experiment destined to be infamous in the annals of education journals, or inspired by George Orwell's *Animal Farm*, but it appeared homerooms in junior high were mixed age, single gender, at least for Division C (not A, the academically capable, or B, farther down the evolutionary scale in terms of brain development, but . . . well, you know what I'm getting at).

One day at the end of lunch break the warning bell (buzzer) sounded. God, I hated that sound. Division C headed to their designated classroom near the front of the school, conveniently located near the administration office, where strappings would occur if necessary. Limey (Mr. Covington) was late to supervise his charge. He was likely trying to get one more smoke in before facing the zoo and possibly contemplating his career path for the umpteenth time. Anyway, think of that Nature Channel special episode on orangutans. No, wait. I don't want to be sued by an orangutan, much less have a class suit filed against me by the whole group of them (there is no term for a group of orangutans since they are mostly solitary animals in nature).

Things were rather rambunctious in the classroom that day, not to the level of that time in French class when the teacher left to make copies of an exercise and returned to find Richard Jones lying under his desk with a broken arm . . . but rambunctious.

One of the older Sweathogs, Lairdy, must have decided to deputize himself, and bring order to this Wild West scene. For some reason, he focused on Gumper, who was clear across the classroom, five rows of desks away.

"Gumper . . . sit down."

"Screw you, Laird!"

"Gumper. I said sit down."

"Piss off, Laird!"

"FINAL WARNING, GUMPER. SIT THE "F" DOWN!"

Gumper ignored Lairdy. As was his custom, Lairdy lifted his hands towards his face mimicking a pair of binoculars and scanned the room before focusing his gaze, with an imaginary adjustment to the imaginary binoculars, on Gump. With an impressive reverberation ("hork") in his throat, nearby bystanders knew there was going to be trouble.

Now I have no idea how to print the sound Lairdy made as he expelled what he expelled. I should imagine if you've ever heard the sound of an Amazonian native firing a dart from his blowgun, 20 paces from his prey, you have an idea of the sound. It is a short sound, and there is simply not enough time for another mammal, the intended recipient, to avoid the inevitable.

The fates abandoned Gumper that day. The well-defined and substantive greeney arched through the air like an outside Oscar Robertson two-pointer. It had a measured pinpoint accuracy that I doubt even Lairdy could have predicted. It was the proverbial hole in one—he hit the sweet spot, Gumper's right cavum concha.

It was another one of those soul-searching, ambivalent moments. I mean, you had to give it to, Lairdy. What a shot! But it was just so gross. Soooo gross.

. . .

Mr. McKellar ran a tight ship. But he had to. When our group, composed of hormone-awakened 13- to 15-year-olds arrived for our first drafting class in the Industrial Education building, pandemonium was in the air. He soon settled us down though, directing us to all take a seat behind a student desk, bringing some organization to the chaos that was our group. He had that special kind of delivery that communicated to your brain that it was time to go to sleep: monotone and repetitive.

The carrot was dangled in front of our noses later during our first class. He led us through a door into the shop! There were all manner of machines, mostly sawdust-covered, indicating that indeed we would be working with wood. Without knowing what some of the machines actually did, I could envision losing a finger or two. Most of us resigned ourselves to the fact that to gain access to machine-land we would have to get through our drafting lessons first, and more or less good behaviour would move things along.

After a few weeks of drafting classes, our introduction to woodwork began. The first few classes in the shop were closely supervised and we were kept close together. It wasn't Mr. McKellar's first rodeo. Our first project involved two pieces of pine wood. We learned how to make a few cuts, do some sanding, apply glue, countersink a few screws, slap on some varnish, and voila, a rudimentary shelf appeared. I know for a fact that many dads received them as birthday gifts, although I am less sure how many of these creations actually were mounted on walls.

Things progressed. Gradually, the projects became more challenging and varied. Eventually, we all got to pick our own project and were granted much more freedom to move about the shop. There were some talented guys in the class. I wasn't one of them. I was barely able to complete my round coffee table, which wasn't particularly round. For years Foo would tell the story of seeing me rolling my table up the hill to my house upon its completion.

Eventually, we moved on to power mechanics. I found it interesting. I'd always wondered what went on in a car's engine and what the various parts did. After a few weeks of seatwork and listening to Mr. McKellar, we were granted access to the automotive shop downstairs.

At some point Mr. McKellar brought an old car into the shop, I guess thinking that it would be an excellent learning activity for his students to take it apart. For about a week, all his power mechanic classes worked on removing the shell of the car. It would be rolled outside of the shop each morning and then rolled back in at the end of the school day. Where wrenches could be used to remove old bolts they were. Otherwise, hammers and cold chisels were utilized to expose the skeleton of the beast.

I don't know what possessed Brad LaFleur. I just remember there were a few of us outside hanging around the car. Mr. McKellar was somewhere in the building. Talk started about whether or not the motor in the car would actually run. Someone connected the battery clamps to the battery. Brad jumped into the one remaining car seat, the driver's seat. There must have been a key in the ignition or he was proficient at hot-wiring, because the next thing we heard was the car come to life. Brad goosed the gas pedal a few times, which resulted in black smoke filling the air. Before you could shake a stick, he popped the clutch and the rear tires spun like crazy. Since there was no weight to the vehicle, the car moved sideways, not forward. We scrambled to avoid meeting our maker. Mr. McKellar was there in a flash, ending the most interesting class we ever had at the Industrial Education building.

· · ·

There were obstacles to getting up close and personal with the girls in junior high. First off, I hadn't transcended my ugly duckling stage. My ears still stuck out. I was skinny and nervous whenever I came in range of a girl. My bespectacled face hardly communicated attractiveness. In short, I would hardly be viewed as boyfriend potential by the attractive girls.

And . . . there was another dynamic at play: the older boys. It would be a busy place in the school's small parking lot afterschool, when several hot cars rolled in: 20-year-old loggers, there to pick up their 15-year-old girlfriends. How could a guy compete?

Bobbi Big Breasts was a case in point. She was an above average looker, attractive beyond the obvious. She'd been snagged by Curly, a monster of a young man. The joke going around was that Curly had better be careful . . . "one slip of the elbows and he'd be up for manslaughter."

At the end of each school day, Curly would be waiting for Bobbi in his American muscle car. How many times did I see her climb into Curly's car trying to engage in conversation with Curly, having to shout to be heard above the exhaust growl? If she'd only let me double her home on my bike, I'd have given her the conversation she deserved.

I had a crush on Samantha. She had beautiful dark hair and she was mature in the right places, so to speak. A big part of me knew that I was out of her league. I don't think I'd even had a conversation with her other than asking if I could borrow a pen from her in Social Studies. But those things didn't deter me from trying to make a move.

She'd been away from school for about a week. I missed seeing her. I decided I had to do something. One evening after dinner when mum and dad were at the barn and Calvin and Lena were parked in front of the television, I snuck upstairs to my parents' bedroom. I'd found her number in the phone book a couple of days earlier and had been carrying it with me, waiting until I had the courage.

Their family's phone rang three times. A woman answered. "Hello."

"Um, hello. Could I speak to Samantha, please?"

There was a pause. "Who is this?" she asked.

I panicked. "Um . . . it's a friend of Samantha's from school."

"Oh, okay. I'll get her for you."

Several minutes went by. My heart went into panic mode. I had plenty of time to realize that I had absolutely no plan about what to say to her.

Finally. "Hello, this is Samantha. Who's this?"

"Um . . . it's Stuey . . . I mean, Stuart. Stuart Moore."

Silence. The seconds ticked. One, two, three, four. "What do you want?"

Now I was in full-blown panic mode. "Um . . . er . . . I hope you're okay. I haven't seen you at school for a while."

More silence. Then, "Yeah. So why did you phone me?"

"Oh, uh, thanks for lending me a pen last week. I really appreciated it."

. . .

Once and awhile I think of her
My memories take me to her
I go back to that place
Back to that time.

The night of the junior-high school dance had started with great anticipation. Cale had organized the purchase of a six pack of Old Style beer through a friend of his older brother's. Unfortunately, he had chosen to drink a couple of bottles before coming to my house to pick me up.

Perhaps Cale smelled of alcohol or my mum's superpowers of knowing all were at work again; regardless my mother declared, "No, Stu is not going with you, Cale."

To which Cale replied, "Ah, c'mon. Let the kid have some fun." Which did not go over—at all.

Cale was sent on his way and I was left fuming, and very unsure as to whether I was going to be attending the dance at all.

In an hour, I was allowed to leave the house. I walked up the trail that ran the length of Moore's Forest. I knew there would be some friends hanging out there. I found Cale, and there were two or three unopened beer bottles left. I drank two bottles relatively quickly, despite the fact that the taste hadn't improved since I was last given a taste of my dad's beer. Up the trail we went, into the school, tickets were handed over, our wrists were stamped, into the gym we went.

The gym was filled with music. Over the course of the hour or so I was at the dance, I think the latest hit, "Sugar Sugar," by the Archies, was played three or four times. The combination of music, a darkened gymnasium, and the alcohol that had kicked in, had me, a reluctant participant in the past at elementary school sock hops, dancing in no time.

I spotted Sally Chapin, a grade "eighter" that Bowser seemed to have his sights on. In fact, I later learned he'd walked her to the dance. I just remember having some dances with Sally and leaving the gym with her about an hour later.

We walked past the hospital and then zigged into the alley behind the Moreland house for some privacy. Halfway down the alley, I found a shed/workshop on the back of someone's property. The door was unlocked. We went in. There were no lights. Perfect!

It's too soon
To tell her yet
I know
But
Impatient love
Won't wait

We were afraid to move around much because we didn't know what we'd bump into or knock over, so we stood face to face, arms wrapped around each other, at times lips to lips. We weren't there long when Sally said she was getting cold. We left shortly thereafter and I walked her home, all the way down to her house past the Home Store. It was a most exciting evening!

I didn't mind the walk home, the first part through the dark, since streetlights were far and few between in the outskirts of the village. I bounded up the hill past the Sunderland Medical Clinic to the level ground where the hospital was situated.

I may be imagining it—perhaps I am touched by nostalgia at this moment—but I truly think I hesitated long enough in front of the hospital to ponder how significant it was. It was the site where the children of Sunderland came into the world, where the citizens of the village received treatment for their ailments, and where many villagers left this earth.

The hospital was also the reason that my family had come to live in the beautiful, beautiful village of Sunderland.

"We shall not cease from exploration
And the end of all our exploring
Will be to arrive where we started
And know the place for the first time."

—T.S. Eliot

Printed in Canada